The Rational Guide To

Google Blogger

PUBLISHED BY

Rational Press - An imprint of the Mann Publishing Group
710 Main Street, 6th Floor
PO Box 580
Rollinsford, NH 03869, USA
www.rationalpress.com
www.mannpublishing.com
+1 (603) 601-0325

ISBN: 0-9726888-7-0
Library of Congress Control Number (LCCN): 2006920359
Printed and bound in the United States of America.
10 9 8 7 6 5 4 3 2 1

Trademarks

Disclaimer of Warranty

Credits

Author:	Wei-Meng Lee
Technical Editor:	Biz Stone
Editorial Director:	Jeff Edman
Book Layout:	Molly Barnaby
Indexer:	Christine Frank
Series Concept:	Anthony T. Mann
Cover Concept:	Marcelo Paiva

All Mann Publishing Group books may be purchased at bulk discounts.

The Rational Guide To

Google
Blogger

Wei-Meng Lee

RATIONAL
PRESS

An imprint of the
www.mannpublishing.com

About the Author

Wei-Meng Lee is a technologist and founder of Developer Learning Solutions, a technology company specializing in hands-on training on the latest Microsoft technologies. Wei-Meng speaks regularly at international conferences and has authored and coauthored numerous books on .NET, XML, and wireless technologies, including *ASP.NET 2.0: A Developer's Notebook* and the *.NET Compact Framework Pocket Guide* (both from O'Reilly Media, Inc.). He writes extensively for trade magazines and online publications on topics ranging from .NET to Mac OS X.

Acknowledgements

Writing a book requires a collective effort of many great individuals and I am indeed honored to be able to work with a team of talented professionals. I would like to take this opportunity to thank Anthony T. Mann for giving me this opportunity to write this book, and a heartfelt thanks to my editor Jeff Edman and Project Coordinator Alison Taber, for their great work in producing this book. And a special thanks to my technical editor Biz Stone, for the invaluable tips and advice.

About Rational Guides

Rational Guides, from Rational Press, provide a no-nonsense approach to publishing based on both a practicality and price that make them rational. Rational Guides are compact books of 224 pages or less. Each Rational Guide is constructed with the highest quality writing and production materials—at a reasonable price. All Rational Guides are intended to be as complete as possible within the 224-page size constraint. Furthermore, all Rational Guides come with bonus materials, such as additional chapters, applications, code, utilities, or other resources. To download these materials, just register your book at www.rationalpress.com. See the instruction page at the end of this book to find out how to register your book.

Who Should Read This Book

This book is intended for anyone who wants to learn how to build their own blog using Google's free Blogger service. This book covers the basic and the not-so-basic concepts and technologies that you need to know in order to thrive in the blogging world. If you are thinking of starting your own blog, look no further, this is the book for you!

With this book, you will learn how to use Blogger's Post Editor and Dashboard to create sophisticated postings that include images and hyperlinks, and how to change the look and feel of your blog using templates. Other topics include making money using Google's AdSense and Amazon.com's Associates program, using photo blogging services, adding a site counter so that you can track your readership, using Blogger Mobile for mobile blogging, and how to archive your blog. For those of you who have your own Web hosting, you will learn how to publish your blog to your own server.

Conventions Used In This Book

The following conventions are used throughout this book:

► *Italics* — First introduction of a term.

► **Bold** — Exact name of an item or object that appears on the computer screen, such as menus, buttons, dropdown lists, or links.

► `Mono-spaced text` — Used to show a Web URL address, computer language code, or expressions as you must exactly type them.

► **Menu1⇨Menu2** — Hierarchical Windows menus in the order you must select them.

Tech Tip:
This box gives you additional technical advice about the option, procedure, or step being explained in the chapter.

Note:
This box gives you additional information to keep in mind as you read.

FREE *Bonus:*
This box lists additional free materials or content available on the Web after you register your book at `www.rationalpress.com`.

⚠ *Caution*
This box alerts you to special considerations or additional advice.

Contents

Contents

Contents

Introduction

Chapter 1

An Introduction to Blogging

Welcome to the world of Blogging! By now, you have probably heard the word "blogging" umpteen times! If you have always wondered what exactly a blog is, this chapter gives you a good overview of blogging. It shows the basics of blogging, as well as some of the jargon that you need to know in order to survive in the blogging world. Subsequent chapters show you how to build your own blog using Google's free Blogger service. So, fasten your seat belt and enjoy the journey!

What is a Blog?

A blog is a collection of periodic articles (known as posts). Here's the definition of a blog from Wikipedia, the free encyclopedia (`http://en.wikipedia.org/wiki/Blog`):

"A blog is website that contains written material, links or photos being posted all the time, usually by one individual, on a personal basis. The term is a shortened form of weblog, although the latter term has since fallen into disuse."

Put simply, a blog is like your online diary, where you update it on a regular basis with information. This information could be facts that you want to share with your readers, or just your incessant raves and rants about something of interest. Blogs are good vehicles for voicing your concerns (where the traditional mediums like newspapers and television might not be sufficiently interested in reporting on them). Blogs are gaining popularity in many countries throughout the world.

If you are a nerd who loves all things technological, you will love Slashdot (`http://slashdot.org`) (see Figure 1.1). Slashdot is an immensely popular technology-related Web site, updated several times daily with links to stories on other Web sites, with the ability to let readers post comments (often controversial ones) for discussions.

Figure 1.1: Slashdot.

Another site similar to Slashdot is BoingBoing (http://www.boingboing.net/), shown in Figure 1.2.

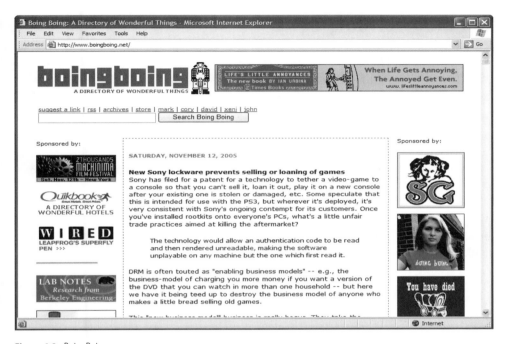

Figure 1.2: BoingBoing.

Besides these specialized blogs focusing on technology, traditional news Web sites such as CNN (http://www.cnn.com) and the New York Times (http://www.nytimes.com/) are also transforming themselves into blogs by providing RSS documents (more on this in the next section) so that readers can subscribe to them.

Note:

Bloglines, a free online service for searching, subscribing, creating, and sharing news feeds, blogs, and rich Web content, maintains a list of top blogs at
http://www.bloglines.com/topblogs.

Blogging Terminologies

Let's briefly define some terms that you will often come across in the world of blogging.

Syndication

The most direct way for a reader to read your blog is to visit your blog site. However, it is a chore to the reader if he has to visit each and every one of the blogs he is interested in (that's a lot of blogs to visit if his interest is broad). A better way would be for your blog to generate an XML document that contains a summary of your blog so that readers can subscribe to it using applications known as *newsreaders*.

When someone says that his blog is *syndicated*, it means that his site produces an XML document containing the summary of his blog. Today, there are two popular XML standards for blog syndication—RSS and Atom. These two standards are discussed in the section "Blog Syndication Standards."

Aggregation

When a blog produces an RSS/Atom document containing a summary of its blog content, newsreaders will retrieve the RSS/Atom document when subscribed to that particular blog. This process of retrieving the RSS/Atom document is known as *aggregation*. Aggregation allows you to quickly glance through the main content of a blog without visiting it. This is in fact one of the greatest advantages blogs have over traditional Web sites. A user who is using a newsreader may subscribe to over 100 blogs, but he can quickly glance through what is new in each blog by simply looking at the content of the RSS/Atom document (which is now formatted nicely by the newsreader for viewing).

Blog Syndication Standards

Figure 1.3 shows some of the icons you will see on Web sites that support blog syndication.

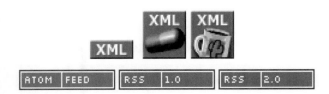

Figure 1.3: Icons for Supported Feeds.

In December 2005, Microsoft announced they had adopted the icon used to represent RSS and syndication related features in Firefox as the standard icon for blog syndication in Internet Explorer 7. You can learn more about this new icon at `http://feedicons.com/`. Figure 1.4 shows the new blog syndication icon.

Figure 1.4: New Blog Syndication Icon.

RSS

RSS is one of the two XML standards used for blog syndication. RSS stands for several things (depending on whom you talk to)—Really Simple Syndication, or Rich Site Summary, or RDF Site Summary.

RSS is an XML document (known as a *feed*) that contains a list of items such as title, description, links, etc. Usually, an RSS document contains an extract of a blog, summarizing its content.

RSS went through a number of revisions over the past few years. There are two camps in the industry: RSS 0.91, 0.92, 0.94, and 2.0 versus RSS 1.0.

- ▶ **RSS 0.91** — Released by Netscape in July 1999.

- ▶ **RSS 0.92** — Upgraded by Dave Winer of UserLand.

- ▶ **RSS 0.94 and 2.0** — Upgraded by Dave Winer of UserLand in August 2002.

- ▶ **RSS (RDF (Resource Description Framework) Site Summary) 1.0**
  — Upgraded by the RSS-DEV Working Group in December 2000.

Figure 1.5 shows what an RSS 2.0 document looks like:

Figure 1.5: RSS Document.

Atom

The evolution of the RSS standards has been a topic of much debate and contention. As an alternative to RSS, a new blog syndication standard known as Atom was developed by a rival group. Blogger supports the Atom syndication standard.

Figure 1.6 shows what an Atom document looks like:

Figure 1.6: Atom Document.

OPML

Besides RSS and Atom, you will sometimes see the word OPML, which stands for Outline Processor Markup Language. An OPML document is an XML document that contains a list of RSS feeds to which you have subscribed. For example, if your friend is subscribed to a list of 20 RSS feeds and highly recommends that you subscribe to them as well, all he needs to do is use his newsreader to export an OPML file and send it to you. You can then import the OPML file and subscribe to the 20 RSS feeds in one go. For a good discussion of RSS and Atom, check out http://en.wikipedia.org/wiki/RSS_%28file_format%29.

Newsreaders

Blogs are popping up like mushrooms. There are simply too many of them for you to find and read on a regular basis. That's why you need a newsreader to aggregate the various blogs into a common area so that you can read them all in one place. In this section, I will share with you my favorite newsreader and discuss some of its features. A good newsreader should have the following features:

▶ A built-in Web browser for following the links in an RSS feed.

▶ Ability to automatically add a feed when it finds one in the Web browser.

RSS Bandit

For my blog aggregation, I use RSS Bandit from `http://www.rssbandit.org/`. You can download the free RSS Bandit from `http://www.rssbandit.org/ow.asp?DownLoad`. RSS Bandit supports both the RSS and Atom standards.

Note:

RSS Bandit requires .NET Framework 1.0/1.1. You can download the free .NET Framework from

`http://msdn.microsoft.com/netframework/downloads/updates/default.aspx.`

Once installed, you will see that RSS Bandit divides the window into three main parts (see Figure 1.7). Your news feeds are on the left. The top right pane of your window displays the blog postings from the feed you have selected on the left. The bottom right pane displays the summary of the posting selected in the top right pane.

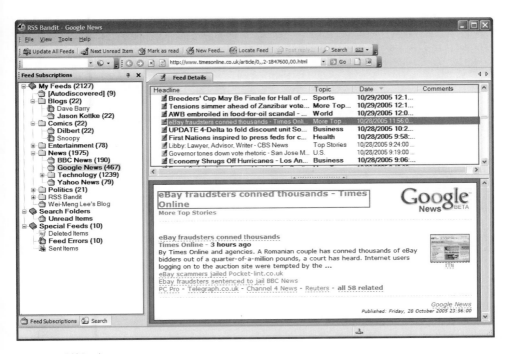

Figure 1.7: RSS Bandit.

To view the detailed posting, click the posting title on the bottom right pane and a new tab will be displayed to show the detailed posting using the built-in Web browser (see Figure 1.8). All this happens within RSS Bandit itself; there is no need to switch between different applications.

Figure 1.8: Viewing a Web Page Using the Built-in Web Browser.

One nice feature of RSS Bandit is the ability to automatically locate feeds from the page you are currently viewing. For example, if you are viewing a page from http://msdn. microsoft.com/, you can simply click the **Locate Feed** button at the top of the window (see Figure 1.9) to look for feeds that are contained in the page.

Figure 1.9: Looking for Feeds from a Page.

A window will pop up to let you choose the Web page to scan from (the current page URL is automatically inserted). Click the **Find Feeds** button (see Figure 1.10).

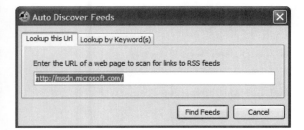

Figure 1.10: Specifying the URL for Feeds.

RSS Bandit will then show a list of feeds that it has found from the page. Select the feed that you want to subscribe to and click the **Subscribe** button (see Figure 1.11).

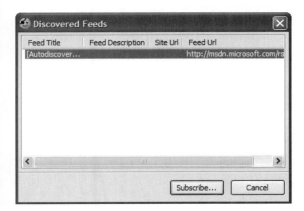

Figure 1.11: Selecting the Feeds Found.

If the title of the feed is not displayed on the window, you can click the **Get title from feed** button to retrieve the title from the page. You can also specify the category to add your feeds to. Click the **OK** button to add the feed to your subscription (see Figure 1.12).

Add New Feed ✕

Url	http://msdn.microsoft.com/rss.xml
Title	MSDN Just Published	Get title from feed
Category	[Unclassified Feeds] ▾

☐ Enable alert windows on received items

Authentication

| Username | |
| Password | |

OK   Cancel

Figure 1.12: Adding a New Feed.

You can configure RSS Bandit to automatically update all your feed subscriptions via the **Feeds** tab (choose the **Tools⇨ Options** menu item). Or you can simply click the **Update All Feeds** button to update all the feeds immediately (see Figure 1.13).

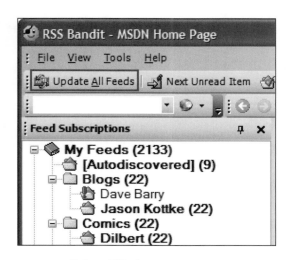

Figure 1.13: Updating All Feeds.

Google Reader

If you prefer to use a Web-based newsreader instead of a Windows-based newsreader like RSS Bandit, you will like the Google Reader (http://www.google.com/reader), shown in Figure 1.14. Google Reader was built by two Googlers who broke off from the Blogger team to build an RSS aggregator.

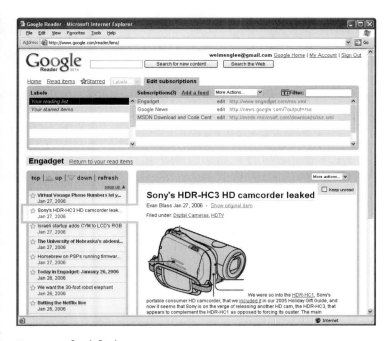

Figure 1.14: Google Reader.

To use the Google Reader, you can create a new account with Google or just use your existing Gmail (or other Google service accounts). The Google Reader integrates tightly with Blogger and you can blog right from the reader. To blog about a particular news item, simply select the **Blog This!** option shown in Figure 1.15. A window will appear and you can now blog directly onto your Blogger account.

Figure 1.15: Blogging Directly from Google Reader.

Creating Your Own Blog

Now that you understand what a blog is and have seen some of the more popular blogs, what about creating one yourself? The good news is that when it comes to blogging, you have many choices, and most of them are free! While this book focuses on using Google's free Blogger service, here are some other choices:

► **WordPress** — http://wordpress.com/

► **Moveable Type** — http://www.movablteype.org/

► **Radio Userland** — http://radio.userland.com/

► **Bloglines** — http://www.bloglines.com/

► **TypePad** — http://www.typepad.com/

► **Blognet** — http://www.blognet.info/

► **LiveJournal** — http://www.livejournal.com/

Summary

In this chapter, you have seen the basics of blogs and some of the technologies that make blogging possible. You've learned the definitions of many of the most common terms in the world of blogging. You have also seen how to use a newsreader to subscribe to blogs that you are interested in. Let's move on to the next chapter to learn how to create your first blog!

Chapter 2

Getting Started with Blogger

The last chapter introduced the world of blogging and several technologies that make this world tick. This chapter shows you how you can create your own blog using Google's free Blogger account. I will use my own personal blog as an example and by the time you reach the end of the next two chapters, you will be able to create your own blog similar to the one shown in Figure 2.1.

Figure 2.1: Create Your Own Blog Using Blogger.

Setting Up an Account

The first step towards setting up your own blog is to register for a free account at `http://www.blogger.com/start` (see Figure 2.2). You can register as many accounts as you like. There is no cost involved.

Figure 2.2: Creating a Blog in Three Easy Steps.

Tech Tip:

If you would like to maintain several blogs (each one with a unique URL), you simply need to create one user account and then add multiple blogs to your account. You will learn more about this in Chapter 4.

Note:

All blogs created and hosted by Blogger have the domain name of
`http://yourblog.blogspot.com.`

Creating a new user account at Blogger is simple. First go to `http://www.blogger.com/start` and click the **Create Your Own Blog Now** button (shown in Figure 2.2), then follow this easy three-step process.

1. In the screen shown in Figure 2.3, supply the following information:

    *   **User name** — Used to uniquely identify you as a registered user of Blogger.

    *   **Password** — The password for your account.

    *   **Display name** — The name to be displayed at the bottom of your post.

    *   **Email address** — Your e-mail address.

Figure 2.3: Creating an Account.

Be sure to read the terms of service and then check the acceptance box if you agree to it. Click the **Continue** button.

2. Give your blog a title and choose the URL you want to use for your blog, as shown in Figure 2.4. In this example, I have chosen `http://weimenglee.` `blogspot.com`. Choose a name you like for your own blog. You should choose a URL that is simple to type and easy for users to remember. You also have the option to host your blog at some other servers, such as your own company's server (see Chapter 7 for more information). To proceed to the next step, click the **Continue** button.

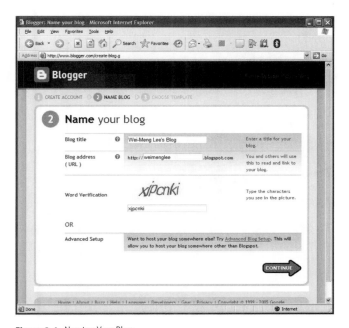

Figure 2.4: Naming Your Blog.

3. Choose a template to use for your blog. A template defines your blog's look
    and feel. You can change the selected template later, as discussed in the
    next section, "Customizing Your Blog." For now, choose the first template
    (Minima, as shown in Figure 2.5) and click the **Continue** button to proceed.

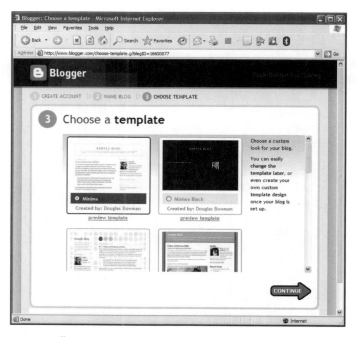

Figure 2.5: Choosing a Template for Your Blog.

That's it! Your blog is now created and ready for your first post. Click the **Start Posting** button to post your first blog entry (see Figure 2.6).

Figure 2.6: Blog Created Successfully.

Your First Post

With your blog created successfully, you can now start posting. To test your first post, give your post a title and then type something into the text area (see Figure 2.7). When you are done, click the **Publish Post** button.

Figure 2.7: Creating Your First Post.

To view your blog, click the **View Blog** tab (see Figure 2.8).

Figure 2.8: Blog Published Successfully.

That's it! You now have your own blog, as shown in Figure 2.9!

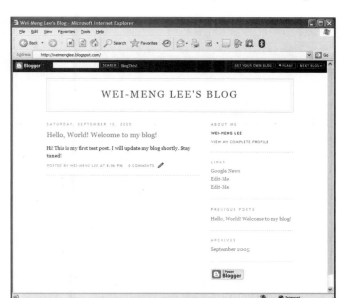

Figure 2.9: Your Own Blog!

Customizing Your Blog

The blog that you have created in the last section is a little plain. This section shows you how to spice things up a little.

The *Dashboard* (shown in Figure 2.10) is the place where you can administer the look and feel of your blog.

1. Access the Dashboard by going to http://www.blogger.com. If you have previously logged in to the Dashboard, you will automatically be redirected to it. If not, you will be prompted to enter your username and password to log in.

Figure 2.10: The Dashboard.

2. In the Dashboard, click the **Wei-Meng Lee's Blog** link to edit the settings of the blog. This will bring you to a screen similar to that shown in Figure 2.7. To change the template of your blog, click the **Template** tab to see the screen in Figure 2.11.

Figure 2.11: Editing the Template.

3. You can modify the template's HTML code if you are comfortable working with HTML and CSS. However, for simplicity in this example, select one of the pre-built templates supplied by Blogger, by clicking the **Pick New** link. You will see a list of templates to choose from, as shown in Figure 2.12.

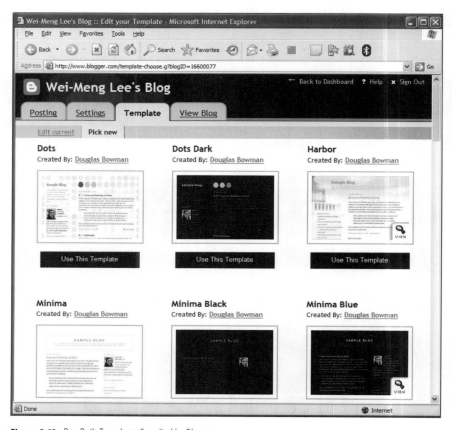

Figure 2.12: Pre-Built Templates Supplied by Blogger.

4.   To preview a template, click on a template that you would like to use (scroll down the page for more templates). For example, if you click on the TicTac Blue template, you should see something similar to Figure 2.13. To apply the selected template to your blog, click the **Use This Template** button located under the template icon.

Figure 2.13: Previewing a Template.

5. Before the template is applied to your blog, you will see a warning dialog (shown in Figure 2.14). When you apply a new template to your blog, all the changes that you have made to the previous template will be lost. Since you have not made any modifications to the template and hence have no changes to lose, click the **OK** button.

Figure 2.14: Previous Customization is Lost When You Choose a New Template.

6. You will now be brought back to the **Template** tab (see Figure 2.15). In order for the template to be applied to your blog, you need to republish it. Click the **Republish** button to republish your blog with the new template.

Tech Tip:

You should always click the Republish button to apply the template to the entire blog immediately. If you click the Republish Index Only button, the new template will not be visible.

Figure 2.15: Republishing Your Blog.

Tech Tip:

Before making any modifications to your template, it's always a good idea to copy the HTML from the form and paste it into a text editing application and save it. That way, if you make a mistake or want to go back to what you had before, you can just paste it back in the form.

That's it! Your blog will now spot the newly selected template, as shown in Figure 2.16.

Figure 2.16: Your Own Blog!

Summary

In this chapter, you have seen how easy it is to create your own blog using Blogger, and how to make your first post. You have also learned how to change the look and feel of your blog using templates. In the next chapter, you will learn how to further customize your blog using the Post Editor.

Chapter 3

Using the Post Editor

In the last chapter, you saw how easy it is to create your own blog using Blogger. You also created your first post. In this chapter, you will learn how to use the Post Editor (a Web-based editor that is part of Blogger) to create more sophisticated postings that includes images as well as hyperlinks.

Adding a New Post

The most common task that you perform on your blog is creating a new post. In Blogger, you can post a message to your blog using the Post Editor by following these steps:

1. Go to the Blogger Dashboard and click on the "+" icon to create a new post to your blog (see Figure 3.1).

Figure 3.1: Adding a Post to Your Blog.

2. The Blogger Post Editor will be displayed, as shown in Figure 3.2. While the Post Editor looks simple, it is actually a very powerful editor for creating nice-looking posts.

Figure 3.2: The Post Editor.

3. The Post Editor supports two view modes: **Edit HTML** mode and **Compose** mode (default), as shown in Figure 3.3.

Figure 3.3: Default Mode of the Post Editor—Compose.

4. In the **Compose** mode, you can simply type your messages just as you would with a word processor such as Microsoft Word. You can also use the various formatting buttons to format your text (see Figure 3.4).

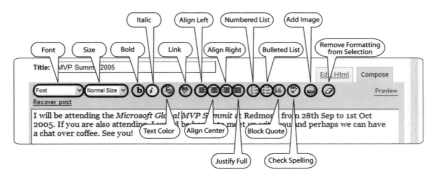

Figure 3.4: Composing a Message.

5. If you prefer to edit your posting in HTML, you can switch to the **Edit HTML** view (see Figure 3.5).

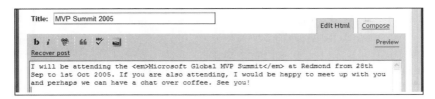

Figure 3.5: Using the Post Editor in HTML Mode.

Tech Tip:

Blogger has a useful "recover post" feature. Writing posts on the Web carries with it some risk of losing a connection or having a browser crash. If this happens while you are in the middle of writing a post in Blogger, navigate back to the new post form and click the **Recover post** item. The last post you were working on will appear.

Spell Checking

The Post Editor supports spell checking, which is a useful tool for ensuring that you don't have a post with too many typos (which doesn't look good to a prospective employer). Click the **Check Spelling** button to bring up the spell checker shown in Figure 3.6.

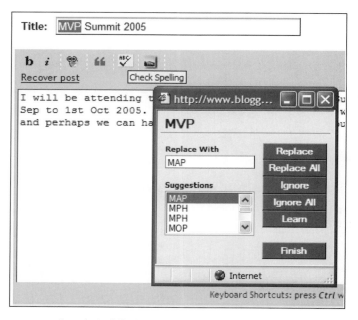

Figure 3.6: Using the Spell Check Feature in the Post Editor.

Tech Tip:

Be sure to turn off any pop-up blocker you might have on your Web browser, or else the spell-check feature will not work.

Creating a Hyperlink

To create a hyperlink, simply highlight the related text and click on the **Link** button to insert the URL to which you will link (see Figure 3.7). You can choose various methods of linking, such as HTTP, FTP, Mailto, and so on.

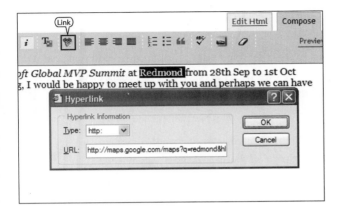

Figure 3.7: Creating a Hyperlink.

Inserting an Image

Follow these steps to insert an image into your post:

1. In the Post Editor, click the **Image** button (see Figure 3.8).

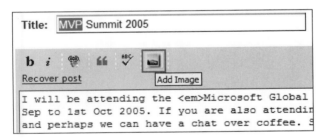

Figure 3.8: Inserting an Image.

2. The window shown in Figure 3.9 appears, allowing you to choose two different ways to use images in your post. The first method is to upload the image from your local computer onto Blogger and then insert the image into your post. This is done by clicking on the **Browse** button to choose the image to upload from the local computer. The second method is to link images from another URL. For example, an image might be stored on another site and instead of downloading the image from that site and uploading it into Blogger, you can directly link to that image from your post.

Tech Tip:

Linking images from another site is not recommended, because every time your post is loaded, the image must be fetched from the remote server, causing the server to consume additional bandwidth in order to display your post.

3. Also in the screen shown in Figure 3.9, you can choose the layout of the image that you are embedding and the size of the image will be automatically adjusted (based on the **Image size** selection of **Small**, **Medium**, or **Large**).

4. To upload the image, click the **Upload Image** button.

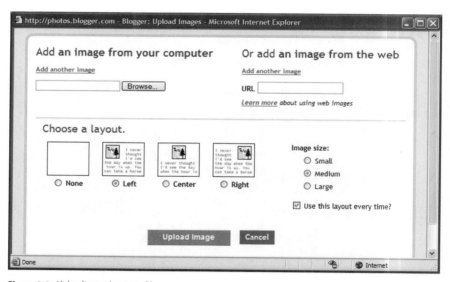

Figure 3.9: Uploading an Image to Blogger.

5. The image will now be embedded in the post (see Figure 3.10).

Figure 3.10: Embedding an Image in the Message.

Publishing the Post

To publish a post, click the **Publish Post** button (shown in Figure 3.11). If you are not ready to publish the post, you can save it as a draft and publish it later. You also have the option to prevent readers of your blog from posting comments on your post. To do so, select the **No** radio button under the **Allow New Comments on This Post** item (see Figure 3.11) You can also change the publish date and time.

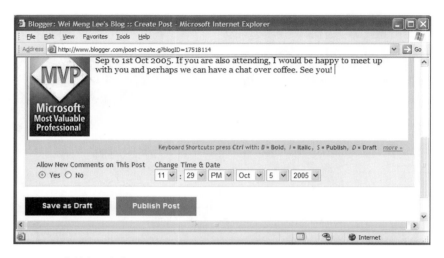

Figure 3.11: Publishing the Post.

When you refresh your blog, you will see the new post, as shown in Figure 3.12.

Figure 3.12: Viewing the New Post.

Post Editor Shortcuts

The Post Editor supports several keyboard shortcuts for editing posts. They work in Internet Explorer 5.5 and above, as well in Web browsers in the Mozilla family (1.6+ and Firefox 0.9+). These shortcuts are:

- ▶ Ctrl + b = Bold

- ▶ Ctrl + i = Italic

- ▶ Ctrl + l = Blockquote (when in HTML-mode only)

- ▶ Ctrl + z = Undo

- ▶ Ctrl + y = Redo

- ▶ Ctrl + shift + a = Link

- ▶ Ctrl + shift + p = Preview

- ▶ Ctrl + d = Save as Draft

- ▶ Ctrl + s = Publish Post

Editing and Deleting a Post

You can edit a previous post by selecting the **Edit posts** link within the **Posting**⇨ **Edit posts** tab (see Figure 3.13). On this page, you will see a list of your previous posts. To make changes to a particular post, click the **Edit** button next to it. To delete a post, click the **Delete** link.

Figure 3.13: Editing and Deleting Previous Postings.

E-mail Your Postings Using Mail-to-Blogger

Besides using the Post Editor to add postings to your blog, you can also post via e-mail, which is actually much easier. Simply send an e-mail to a specific e-mail account in Blogger and your post will be posted automatically. To configure Blogger for e-mail posting, follow these steps:

1. Go to the **Settings**⇨ **Email** tab, as shown in Figure 3.14.

Figure 3.14: Configuring Mail-to-Blogger.

2. In the **Mail-to-Blogger Address** section, enter a secret name in the text box. Collectively, your username and this secret name will be the e-mail address that you will send to when you want to post by e-mail. To enable e-mail posting, check the **Publish** check box.

Caution:

Ensure that you are the only one to know this secret name. If someone else knows about this secret name, he can impersonate you and post on your behalf.

3. The **BlogSend Address** text box allows you to specify an e-mail address so that whenever you publish a post, an e-mail is sent to the specified address. I suggest you enter your own e-mail address so that you can be notified of the posts you have in your blog (just in case someone knows about your secret name and posts on your behalf).

4. Click the **Save Settings** button to save the settings.

5. Let's now try to send an e-mail to add a new post. Using your favorite e-mail client (I used Outlook Express in this example), compose an e-mail (see Figure 3.15) and send it to the e-mail address you specified earlier.

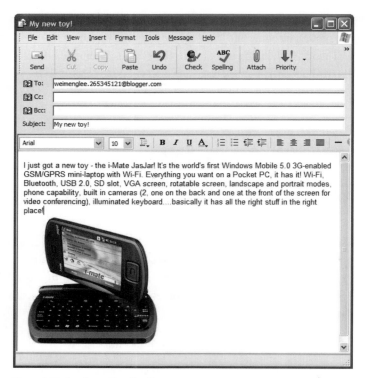

Figure 3.15: Sending an E-mail to Blogger.

6. To view the new posting, refresh your blog and you should now see the new posting (see Figure 3.16). At the same time, you will receive an e-mail notifying you that you have just posted a new entry to your blog.

Figure 3.16: Viewing the Post.

> ## Note:
> E-mail attachments do not work for Mail-to-Blogger, so you need to embed images into your message. For posting images via attachments, please see Chapter 8.

Instant Blogging Using BlogThis!

When you are surfing the Web and come across something interesting that you want to blog about, you can directly blog it (without needing to use the Post Editor in the Blogger Dashboard) using the BlogThis! tool from Blogger. The BlogThis! tool can be found in the Google Toolbar (see `http://toolbar.google.com/`).

Tech Tip:
There is also a separate version of BlogThis! independent of the Google Toolbar. It's a bookmarklet that works with any browser. All you have to do is drag it into your browser's toolbar from this page: http://help.blogger.com/bin/answer.py?answer=152.

To enable BlogThis!, follow these steps:

1. Select the **Options** menu item in Google Toolbar, as shown in Figure 3.17.

Figure 3.17: Google Toolbar.

2. In the **More** tab, check the **BlogThis!** check box (see Figure 3.18) and click the **OK** button.

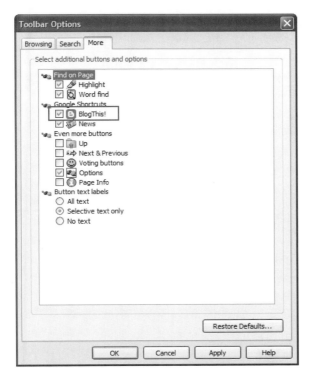

Figure 3.18: Enabling BlogThis!

3.   The BlogThis! icon will now appear in the Google Toolbar (see Figure 3.19).

Figure 3.19: The BlogThis! Icon in the Google Toolbar.

4.   To use the BlogThis! tool, simply surf to a site of interest and then click the BlogThis! icon. If you are not logged in to Blogger, you will be asked to log in.

5.   Once logged in, BlogThis! will use the title of the Web page as the title of your post and then insert a link to the page into the body of your post (see Figure 3.20). Click **Publish** to publish the post.

Figure 3.20: Blogging about the Current Page.

6. You can now view the post by clicking the **VIEW BLOG** button (see Figure 3.21).

Figure 3.21: Finishing the Post.

Figure 3.22 shows the newly published post.

Figure 3.22: Viewing the Post.

Blogger for Word Add-In

Google has recently released the Blogger for Word Add-in that allows users to publish their post in Blogger via Microsoft Word. Using the Blogger for Word Add-in, you will be able use Microsoft Word to do the following:

▶ Publish to your blog

▶ Save drafts

▶ Edit posts

You can download the Blogger for Word add-in from `http://buzz.blogger.com/` `bloggerforword.html`. Once downloaded and installed, you will see an additional toolbar in Microsoft Word (see Figure 3.23). Blogger for Word can also be downloaded here: `http://www.google.com/downloads/`.

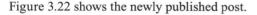

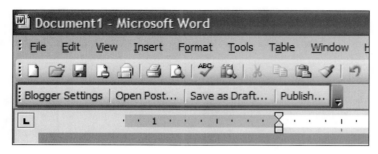

Figure 3.23: Blogger for Word Add-In Toolbar.

You can configure your Blogger account by clicking the **Blogger Settings** button. Figure 3.24 shows the **Settings** dialog for you to enter your Blogger account information.

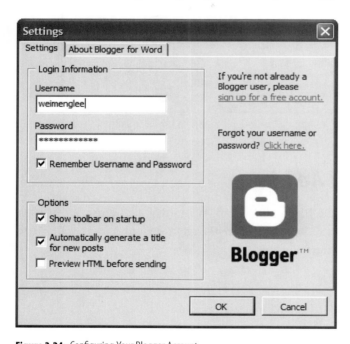

Figure 3.24: Configuring Your Blogger Account.

You can also open your postings in Blogger using the Blogger for Word Add-in by clicking the **Open Post** button. The **Edit Post** dialog will then display the list of posts available (see Figure 3.25). Select the post you want to edit in Word and click the **OK** button.

Figure 3.25: Editing Posts from Blogger.

To create a new post, type your text in Word and then click the **Publish** button (see Figure 3.26). Click the **Send** button to publish this post.

Tech Tip:
Type the title of your post in the first line and the content of your post in a new line. Blogger for Word will then automatically use the first line as the title of the Post and the rest as the content of the post.

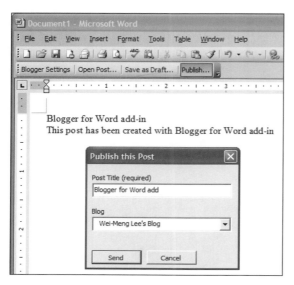

Figure 3.26: Publishing a Post.

You can preview the new post by clicking the **Click here to view your post on the web** link in the **Published** dialog (see Figure 3.27).

Figure 3.27: The Published Dialog.

If you make changes to the text content in Word, you can republish the post. You now have the choice to update the original post, or publish the current content as a new post (see Figure 3.28).

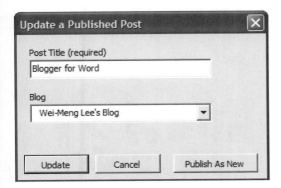

Figure 3.28: Republishing the Post.

Summary

In this chapter, you have seen how you can make a post using the Blogger Post Editor, and how to post via e-mail. Besides posting plain text, you learned how to spice up your post by adding images. You learned the Post Editor shortcuts that will prove very handy, and you saw how to use tools like BlogThis! and the Blogger for Word Add-in.

Did you know?

The Post Editor supports several keyboard shortcuts that you can use while editing your posts. These shortcuts can greatly improve your productivity.

Using Blogger

Chapter 4

Modifying Your Blog Settings

The Blogger Dashboard is the central location where you can change the settings of your blog. In this chapter, you will learn how to use the Dashboard to perform such tasks as adding a photo to your profile, creating, editing, and deleting blog postings, and how to add blogs to your Blogger account.

Describing Your Blog

In the **Settings**⇨ **Basic** tab, you can give your blog a description by filling in the **Description** box (see Figure 4.1). To save the changes, click the **Save Settings** button and then the **Republish** button to republish your blog.

Figure 4.1: Giving Your Blog a Description.

The description will now appear under the **About** header in the sidebar (see Figure 4.2).

Figure 4.2: Viewing the About Section in the Sidebar.

Showing E-mail Post Links

Under the **Settings**⇨ **Basic** tab, there is an option named **Show Email Post Links**. By default, this is set to **No**. You should set this to **Yes** so that readers can easily forward your posting to a friend through e-mail. If this option is set to **Yes**, you will see the e-mail icon located at the bottom of the post (see Figure 4.3).

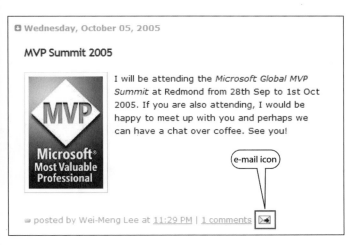

Figure 4.3: E-mail Icon at the Bottom of a Post.

When the e-mail icon is clicked, a reader of your blog will be able to forward your post to another friend through e-mail (see Figure 4.4).

Figure 4.4: Using E-mail to Send a Post to Another Reader.

Editing Your Profile

You can display your personal profile on your blog so that readers can get to know you better. To edit your profile, go to the Dashboard and click the **Edit Profile** link (see Figure 4.5).

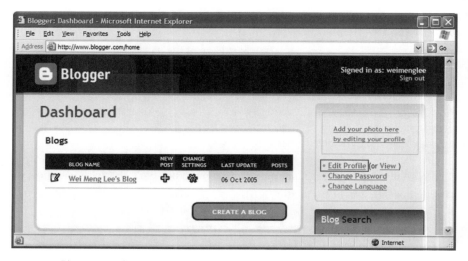

Figure 4.5: Editing Your Profile.

There are several fields to fill in. For simplicity, let's fill in the following fields:

► First Name: Wei-Meng

► Last Name: Lee

► About Me: I am an author and trainer specializing in Microsoft and Mac OS X technologies. I am also a Microsoft .NET Compact Framework MVP.

Click the **Save Profile** button to save the changes. When you refresh your blog, your name and description would be displayed as shown in Figure 4.6.

Figure 4.6: Using Your Profile on Your Blog.

Adding a Photo

In the **Edit Profile** page, you can add a photograph of yourself by clicking on the **Add your photo here by editing your profile** link (see Figure 4.7).

Figure 4.7: Adding a Photo to Your Profile.

However, you will notice that you can only supply the URL of your photo (see Figure 4.8), which means that your photo must be hosted on a server. You can use free photo hosting services such as Hello to host your photo. See Chapter 5 for more information.

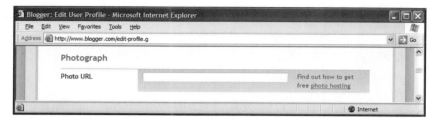

Figure 4.8: Supply a URL Containing Your Photo.

If you just want to upload a photo of yourself without using any photo hosting services, here is a quick fix:

1. Go to the **Posting⇨ Create** page to create a new posting.

2. Insert an image into the post as described in the section "Inserting an Image" in Chapter 3. This will allow you to upload an image (your photo) from your local computer onto Blogger. When the image has finished loading, switch the Post Editor to **Edit HTML** mode. You should be able to see the URL for the uploaded image (see Figure 4.9).

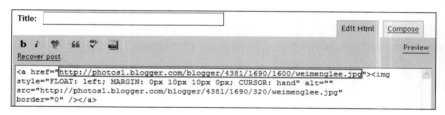

Figure 4.9: Locating the URL for the Uploaded Photo.

3. Copy the highlighted URL and paste it into the **Photo URL** text box (as shown in Figure 4.8) and then save the settings. To view your photo, refresh your blog (see Figure 4.10). You may not immediately see the photo on your blog. If that is the case, try refreshing your blog again later.

Figure 4.10: Viewing the Photo Next to Your Profile.

Deleting Comments

By default, readers can post comments on your blog. While this is a great way to foster interaction and share knowledge between readers and yourself, it has the same side effect as e-mails—it opens the door to unwanted comments and posts. If you click on the links at the bottom of a post, you can see the comments made by readers of your blog (see Figure 4.11).

Figure 4.11: Viewing Comments Made by Readers.

If you do not like the comments made by a reader, you can delete the comments by clicking the **Delete** icon (see Figure 4.12). You need to log in to Blogger to see the **Delete** icon.

Figure 4.12: Deleting Comments.

Configuring Comments

You can customize how comments are handled in the **Settings**⇨ **Comments** page. On this page, you can configure the following (see also Figure 4.13):

▶ **Hide or show Backlinks** — The Backlinks feature makes use of Blog Search to find and display comments from around the Web that others have made about a particular post.

▶ **Hide or show comments** — Comments submitted by readers can be hidden so that you are the only one who can view the comments.

▶ **Who can comment** — You can restrict the ability to make comments to registered users of Blogger, anyone, or only registered members of your blog.

Figure 4.13: Configuring How Comments to Your Blog Are Handled.

Blogger has one interesting feature that you can use to prevent automated systems from spamming your blog. This is done with the **Show word verification for comments** option. When you set this option to **Yes**, the next time a reader posts a comment, he must type the characters he sees in the picture located in the comments page (see Figure 4.14).

Figure 4.14: Word Verification to Prevent Comment Spamming.

Editing Links

By default, the TicTac Blue template sidebar contains a section called **Links**. This section allows you to include links to your favorite sites on your blog. The first one is created for you—Google News (see Figure 4.15). The next two links are placeholders for you to modify.

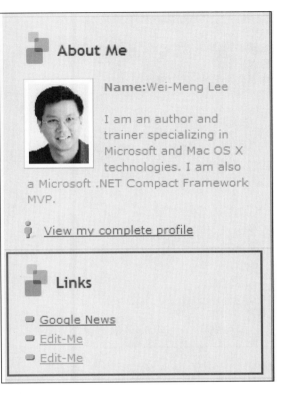

Figure 4.15: Links Section of the Templates Sidebar.

To modify the link placeholders to point to your own favorite Web sites, go to the **Template**⇨ **Edit current** page and scroll through the HTML code until you reach the section highlighted in Figure 4.16.

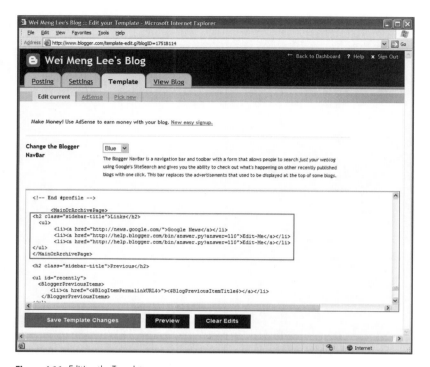

Figure 4.16: Editing the Template.

To link to some other sites, simply modify the <a> elements. For example, the following piece of code will link to Google News, Google Maps, and Amazon.com:

```
<ul>
    <li><a href="http://news.google.com/">Google News</a></li>
    <li><a href="http://http://maps.google.com/">Google Maps</a></li>
    <li><a href="http://www.amazon.com/">Amazon.com</a></li>
</ul>
```

Listing 4.1: Linking Sites.

Save the template by clicking the **Save Template Changes** button and then republish your blog. You will now see the updated links (see Figure 4.17).

Figure 4.17: New Links on Your Blog.

Creating Feeds

Now that you have a blog, you want your readers to be able to subscribe to your blog using RSS aggregators (such as NewsMonster, NewzCrawler, NewsGator, NetNewsWire, Shrook, RSSOwl and BottomFeeder), as discussed in Chapter 1. In order for these aggregators to subscribe to your blog, they need a "feed" from your blog so that they know where to look for new postings. Fortunately, Blogger automatically generates a feed for you without needing you to do anything. Blogger uses Atom for site feed. You can enable or disable Blogger's ability to publish your site feed by following these steps:

1. Go to the **Settings**⇨ **Site Feed** page (see Figure 4.18).

Figure 4.18: Configuring Site Feed.

2. While some aggregators can automatically detect the Atom feed when they visit a blog, it is customary to provide a link on the blog to indicate the existence of the feed. A good way is to put the link in the sidebar of your blog. To do so, go to the **Template**⇨ **Edit current** page and locate the appropriate section to insert the following block of code:

```
<!-- Begin #sidebar -->
    <div id="sidebar">
      <center>
        <a href="<$BlogSiteFeedUrl$>" title="Atom feed">
          <img src="http://photos1.blogger.com/
⊃blogger/4381/1690/1600/atom_icon.gif" />
        </a>
      </center>
      <h2 class="sidebar-title">About</h2>
```

Listing 4.2: Indicating a Feed.

> **Note:**
> This example assumes that you have already uploaded an image of the Atom feed to Blogger (`http://photos1.blogger.com/blogger/4381/1690/1600/atom_icon.gif`). See the section "Adding a Photo" in this chapter for instructions on how to do this.

3. Save the template and republish the blog. Your sidebar will now include an Atom feed link, as shown in Figure 4.19.

Figure 4.19: Adding an Atom Feed Link.

Creating Multiple Blogs

Blogger allows you to create multiple blogs in one single user account. This is useful if you have different areas of interest and want to have different blogs to cater to different audiences.

To add a new blog, go to the Blogger Dashboard and click the **Create a Blog** button (see Figure 4.20).

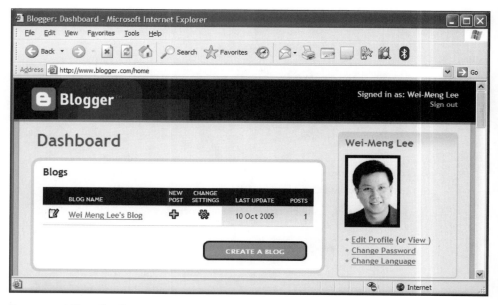

Figure 4.20: Adding a New Blog.

You will be prompted to enter the usual information, such as the name of the new blog, and so on. Once the new blog is created, you will be able to see the new blog in the Dashboard (see Figure 4.21).

Figure 4.21: New Blog in Dashboard.

Deleting a Blog

To delete a blog, follow these steps:

1. Go to the Dashboard and select a blog that you want to delete.

2. Go to the **Settings**⇨ **Basic** page.

3. Scroll to the bottom of the page and click the **Delete this Blog** button (see Figure 4.22).

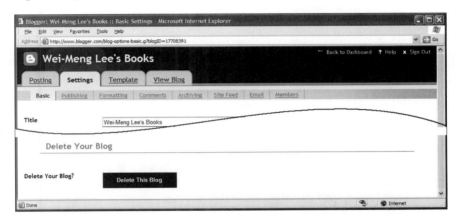

Figure 4.22: Deleting a Blog.

Adding Team Members to Your Blog

By default, you are the only administrator of your blog. However, there are times when it is useful to have more than one person posting to the blog. For example, you might run a blog for your company and you would like a select group of employees to participate in the blog. In this case, you need to add team members to your blog so that different people can post to the same blog.

To add team members to your blog, follow these steps:

1. Go to the **Settings**⇨ **Members** page and click the **Add Team Member(s)** button (see Figure 4.23).

Figure 4.23: Adding New Team Members to the Blog.

2. Add the e-mail addresses of user(s) that you want to add to your blog.

3. When done, click the **Save Settings** button (see Figure 4.24).

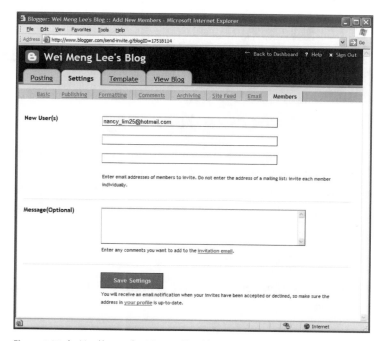

Figure 4.24: Inviting Users to Participate in Your Blog.

4. An invitation e-mail will be sent to the invited users. In the meantime, a list
    of invited users is displayed on the page (see Figure 4.25).

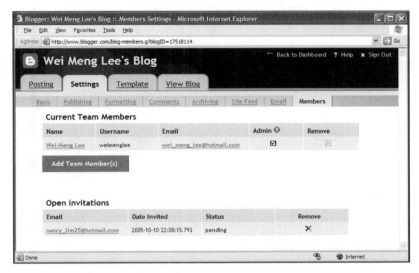

Figure 4.25: List of Users Invited to Your Blog.

Here is an example of an invitation e-mail:

```
From :  Blogger Invites <no-reply@blogger.com>
Sent :  Tuesday, October 11, 2005 5:02 AM
To :  nancy_lim25@hotmail.com
Subject :  Blogger blog invitation from Wei-Meng Lee


Wei-Meng Lee wrote:


null
---------------------------------------


You have been invited by Wei-Meng Lee to join a blog called Wei
MengLee's Blog


Blogger is a free service for easily communicating and sharing ideas
on the web.
```

Next Steps:

1. Please follow the link below. If you do not follow this link, you will not be able to log on to the correct blog.

http://www.blogger.com/i.g?invID=2986939940088215333&hl=en

Note: If this link wraps in your email (not all of it is on one line) copy and paste the entire link into your browser's location bar. Be sure to include characters that may have wrapped to the next line.

2. If you already have a Blogger account, you will be asked to either accept of decline this invitation.

3. If you do not have a Blogger account, you can create one for free in less than a minute. Just click the link and press the 'Create an Account' button.

Thanks!

5. When the user clicks on the link shown in Step 1, the **Join a Blog** page will appear (see Figure 4.26). In order to join the blog, the user must be a registered user of Blogger.

Figure 4.26: Responding to an Invitation from Blogger.

6. Once the user signs in to Blogger, he will see the name of the Blog he is invited to participate in (see Figure 4.27). Notice that by default he is only allowed to add new post to the blog; he is not allowed to make changes to the blog settings (as seen in the disabled **Change Settings** icon).

Figure 4.27: Members Can Add New Posts But Cannot Change the Blog Settings.

7. In your **Settings**⇨ **Members** page, you will see that the user you have invited is now a member of your blog team (see Figure 4.28). To make her an administrator (thereby allowing her to make changes to the blog settings), check the **Admin** check box. To delete the user, click the **Remove** button (represented by an "x").

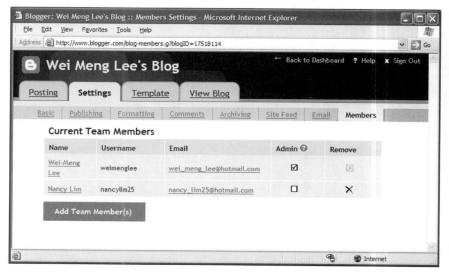

Figure 4.28: Viewing the Team Members List.

Summary

In this chapter, you have seen how you can customize the settings of your blog. In particular, you learned how to customize the sidebar of your blog to display personal information as well as links to other sites and blogs. In addition, you learned how to add new blogs to your accounts and invite members to your blog.

Chapter 5

Photo Blogging

Besides posting messages to your blog, it is also common to post pictures. This is especially true if you are an avid fan of photography and want to share your pictures with fellow blog readers. In Chapter 3 you saw how to insert an image into a post, but it is not very convenient to manually insert individual images. Moreover, there is a size limit to how many photos you can upload to Blogger.

Tech Tip:
Officially, Blogger allows up to 300 MB of photos to be uploaded. But because Blogger automatically resizes each photo to take up minimal space on their servers, users have an unknown (but still limited) amount of photo uploads with every account.

There are some external sites that specifically cater to photo sharing. And best of all, most of them support blogging your photos in Blogger. This chapter shows you four photo blogging services—Picasa, Hello BloggerBot, Flickr, and FotoFlix. These services offer much more than the basic service of hosting photos—you can also organize your photos and add annotations to them.

Picasa

Picasa is an application that helps you instantly manage all the pictures on your PC. Each time you run Picasa, it automatically locates all your pictures (even ones you forgot you had) and sorts them into visual albums organized by date, with folder names you will recognize. You can even drag and drop pictures to arrange your albums and make labels to create new groups. You can download Picasa from `http://picasa.google.com/index.html`.

When Picasa runs for the first time, it will offer to scan your entire computer for pictures, or you can limit the search to only the Desktop, My Documents, and My Pictures folders (see Figure 5.1).

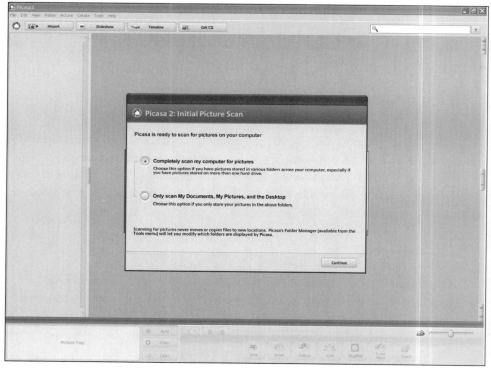

Figure 5.1: Picasa Scanning Your Computer for Pictures.

Once the search is complete, Picasa will show the pictures that were found (see Figure 5.2).

Figure 5.2: Pictures Located by Picasa.

To publish a picture to your blog using Picasa, follow these steps:

1. Select the picture and click the **BlogThis!** button at the bottom of the window (see Figure 5.3).

Figure 5.3: Blogging a Picture.

2. You will be asked to sign in to Blogger if you have not done so. Once you have signed in, you will now see the Post Editor displaying the picture that you have selected. You can add some comments to the picture (see Figure 5.4). When done, click the **Publish** button to publish the post.

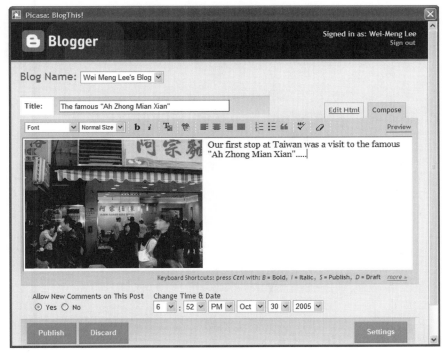

Figure 5.4: Post Editor Displaying the Selected Picture.

3.   Your blog will now contain the new posting (see Figure 5.5).

Figure 5.5: Viewing the Published Post in Blogger.

Hello BloggerBot

Part of Picasa, Hello BloggerBot (http://www.hello.com/index.php) is an application that posts pictures directly onto your blog. You can download Hello BloggerBot from https://secure.hello.com/download.php. Before proceeding to download, you will need to register for a new account.

While you can use Picasa to post pictures to your blog, using Hello BloggerBot is much more convenient if you simply want to post a picture with a short caption, as shown in the following steps:

1. Once Hello is installed on your computer, log in using the account that you have just created, as shown in Figure 5.6.

Figure 5.6: Logging in to Hello.

2. Once you have logged in successfully, you will see the window shown in Figure 5.7. To use BloggerBot, click the **BloggerBot** item shown in the left-hand window and click the **BloggerBot** icon shown on the right.

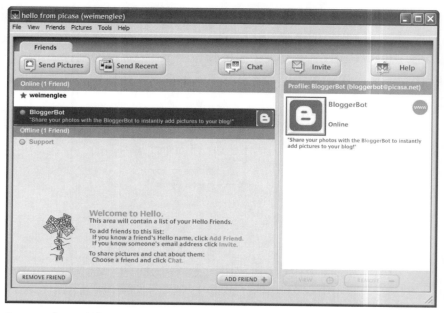

Figure 5.7: Running Hello.

3. You first need to log in to your Blogger account (see Figure 5.8) by clicking the **Sign In** button. Note that this account is not the same as your Hello account.

Figure 5.8: Logging in to Blogger.

4.   If you are using Hello for the first time, you will be asked to configure the settings that Hello should use (see Figure 5.9). In this screen, you can specify:

►   The size of the inline image

►   The size of the archived image

►   The order of the caption

►   The size of the border

Figure 5.9: Configuring Hello for Blogger for the First Time.

5.   You can also append an attribution to the end of each post, indicating whether the picture was posted by Hello, Picasa, none, or others. Click the **Save** button to save the settings.

6. To post a picture to Blogger, simply drag and drop the picture(s) you want to post onto Hello (see Figure 5.10). Select the picture you want to post and then type a caption and click the **Publish** button.

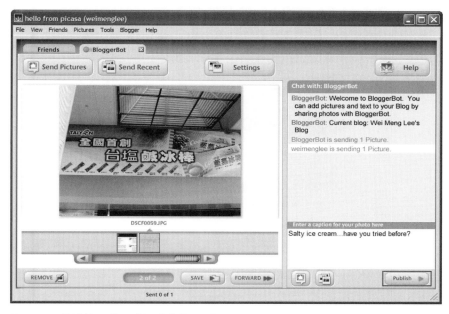

Figure 5.10: Publishing a Photo Using Hello BloggerBot.

The picture will be posted to your blog with the caption specified (see Figure 5.11).

Figure 5.11: Viewing the Published Post in Blogger.

Flickr

Flickr is a digital photo sharing Web site developed by Ludicorp. In March 2005, both Flickr and Ludicorp were bought by Yahoo. You can sign up for a free Flickr account at `http://flickr.com/`.

You can upload your photos through the Web site at `http://www.flickr.com/photos/upload/`, or you can use the upload tool (called Uploadr) provided by Flickr if you have lots of photos to upload. You can download the upload tool at `http://www.flickr.com/tools/`.

Here's how to use Flickr:

1. Once Uploadr is downloaded and installed on your computer, you will be asked for authorization (see Figure 5.12) so that you can start to upload photos to Flickr. Click the **Authorize** Button.

Figure 5.12: Authorizing Uploadr to Upload Photos to Flickr.

2. On the Web page that is shown, click the **OK, I'LL ALLOW IT** button to authorize the upload (see Figure 5.13). Back in Uploadr, click the **Continue** button.

Figure 5.13: Authorizing the Upload.

3. You are now ready to drop photos onto Uploadr so that they can be uploaded to Flickr (see Figure 5.14).

Figure 5.14: Drop Photos to Uploadr for Uploading to Flickr.

4. When you drop large photos onto Uploadr, it will prompt you to resize the photos so that it will save time and bandwidth. You can resize the photo to two different sizes (see Figure 5.15).

Figure 5.15: Resizing Large Photos.

5.   When you are ready to upload the photos to Flickr, click the **Upload** button (see Figure 5.16).

Figure 5.16: Ready to Upload to Flickr.

6. You can assign tags to the photos that you are uploading (see Figure 5.17). For example, if the photos you are uploading were taken during a trip, you might want to assign some meaningful names (such as "Taiwan Trip") so that you can later search for these photos using the assigned tag. You can also create a new set for your photos so that they can be logically organized (click the **Create Set** button to create a new set). By default, your uploaded photos are visible to the public, but you can set it to **Private** if you wish to restrict viewing to selected groups of people. Click the **Finish** button to upload the photos.

Figure 5.17: Configuring the Photos to Be Uploaded.

7. Once the photos are uploaded, click the **See Photos** button to view the uploaded photos (see Figure 5.18).

Figure 5.18: Photos Uploaded Successfully.

8. Figure 5.19 shows the photos that were successfully uploaded to Flickr. You can assign a description to each photo as well as modify their tags. When done, click the **OK** button at the bottom of the page.

Figure 5.19: Viewing the Uploaded Photos.

9. Your photos will be displayed as shown in Figure 5.20. To view an individual photo, click on the photo.

Figure 5.20: Viewing an Individual Photo.

10. Above the photo, you will see the option named **Blog This** (see Figure 5.21). This option allows you to blog your photo directly in Blogger. Click on this option and you will see the message shown in Figure 5.21. Click the **do that now** link to set Flickr to configure Blogger as your blog.

Figure 5.21: Blogging a Photo.

11. You will be asked to select the kind of weblog you have. Select **Blogger Blog** (see Figure 5.22) and click the **Next** button.

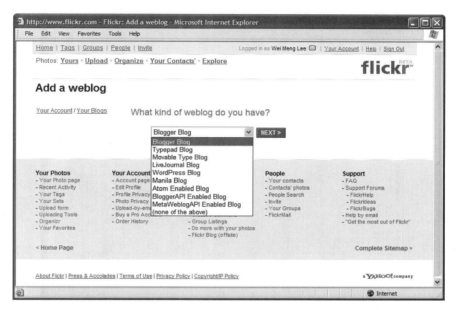

Figure 5.22: Selecting the Type of Weblog.

12. Enter the username and password for your Blogger account (see Figure 5.23), and click the **Next** button.

Figure 5.23: Entering the Credentials for Blogger.

13. Enter the URL and label for your blog and click the **All Done** button (see Figure 5.24).

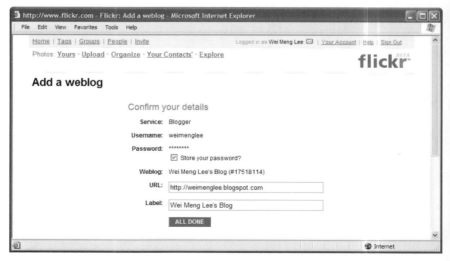

Figure 5.24: Entering Details of Your Blog.

14. That's it! Your Blogger account is configured. To return to the photo that you selected earlier, click the **return to the photo you were blogging** link (see Figure 5.25).

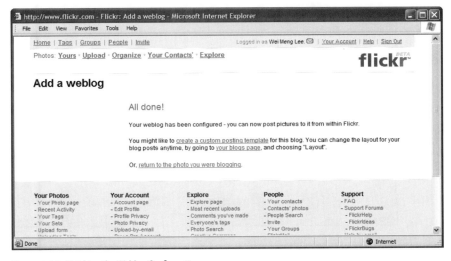

Figure 5.25: Finishing the Weblog Configuration.

Tech Tip:

You can click the **create a custom posting template** link to customize the layout for your blog post.

15. You can now assign a title as well as some text to accompany the photo that you want to blog (see Figure 5.26). Click the **Post Entry** button when done.

Figure 5.26: Assigning a Title to a Photo.

16. You will receive a confirmation note that your photo has been posted on your blog. Click the **take a look at your blog** link to view the photo in Blogger (see Figure 5.27).

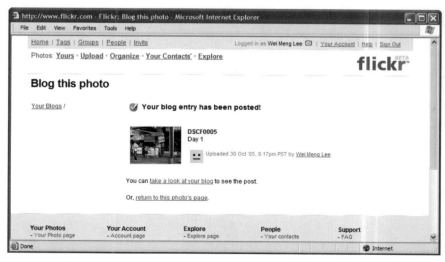

Figure 5.27: Photo Successfully Blogged.

17. Figure 5.28 shows the photo you have just blogged.

Figure 5.28: Viewing the Photo in Blogger.

Adding Notes

One of the great features of Flickr is its ability to add notes to your photo. Figure 5.29 shows a photo displayed in Flickr. When you click on the **Add Note** option at the top of the photo, you will be able to specify a region on your photo and add a note to it. This is useful if you want to add annotations to a photo. In Figure 5.29 I have highlighted the driver of the coach and then added a note: "Our friendly coach driver!"

Figure 5.29: Adding Annotations to a Photo.

If you were to blog this photo on Blogger, it would appear without the note (see Figure 5.30).

Figure 5.30: Viewing the Photo in Blogger.

But if you click on the photo, it will bring you to Flickr. Hover your mouse over the driver and you will now see the note (see Figure 5.31).

Figure 5.31: Viewing the Annotation in Flickr.

Flickr Badges

With the growing popularity of Flickr, there are now Flickr badges that are becoming very popular with Blogger users. A Flickr badge looks like a normal badge that you wear at work, except that it publicizes that you are a user of Flickr. You can create a Flickr badge for yourself at http://flagrantdisregard.com/flickr/badge.php. You just need to enter the information that you want others to know, supply a photo, and then click the **Create badge** button (see Figure 5.32).

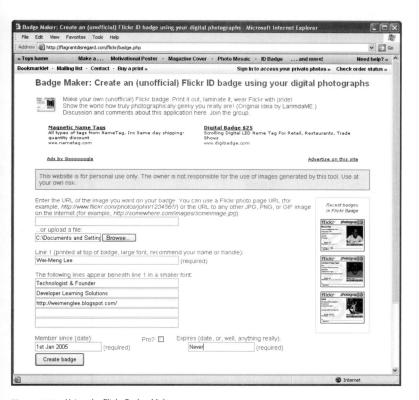

Figure 5.32: Using the Flickr Badge Maker.

Your badge will be created instantly. You can automatically upload the image to your Flickr account (click the link at the bottom of Figure 5.33), or right-click on the badge and save it to your local drive.

Figure 5.33: Viewing the Created Flickr Badge.

You can print the badge and wear it, or embed the badge into the sidebar of your blog and link to your Flickr photo stream. Chapter 4 shows you how to modify the sidebar of your blog.

FotoFlix

FotoFlix (http://www.fotoflix.com/) is another digital photo sharing Web site similar to Flickr. You can register for a free FotoFlix account at https://www.fotoflix.com/ ?action=home.registration_form_b&. Once you have registered, you will receive an activation e-mail from FotoFlix.

Once your FotoFlix account is activated, you can start to upload your photos onto FotoFlix by following these steps:

1. To upload photos, click the **Upload Fotos** button (see Figure 5.34).

Figure 5.34: Uploading Photos to FotoFlix.

2. Unlike Flickr, where you need to download a separate application to upload the photos, you can use the FotoFlix uploader that will be hosted within your Web browser. In Figure 5.35, click the icon for your Web browser to install the uploader in your Web browser.

Figure 5.35: Installing FotoUploader on Your Web Browser.

3. You will be asked to install the ImageUploader2.cab file in your Web
    browser. Once the uploader is installed, you will be able to select the photos
    that you want to upload by dragging the photos from the upper pane and
    dropping them onto the lower pane (see Figure 5.36). Click the **Upload**
    button to upload the selected photos.

Figure 5.36: Dragging and Dropping Photos to Upload.

4. Figure 5.37 shows your uploaded photos. To blog a photo to your blog, click the photo.

Figure 5.37: Photos Uploaded Successfully.

5.   Click the **Blog Foto** button to post the photo onto your blog (see Figure 5.38).

Figure 5.38: Blogging a Photo Using FotoFlix.

6. You can select the blog provider (Blogger in this case), as well as your username, password, and blog URL. In addition, give your photo a title and a description. Click the **Blog Foto** button when done (see Figure 5.39).

Figure 5.39: Specifying the Weblog to Blog the Photo.

Figure 5.40 shows the photo displayed in Blogger.

Figure 5.40: Viewing the Photo in Blogger.

Summary

In this chapter, you have seen how photo blogging works. For photo blogging, you have many choices: there are several photo blogging services and this chapter has covered the four most popular—Picasa, Hello BloggerBot, Flickr, and FotoFlix. Best of all, all these services offer basic functionality for free. So, get that digital camera off your shelf and start photo blogging today!

Did you know?

Blogger has a limit of 300 MB for uploaded photos. But you should not worry about running out of space. Each uploaded photo will be resized so that it takes up minimal space on the servers.

Chapter 6

Generating Revenue with Blogger

If you have been blogging for a while and updating your blog frequently, you may have a steady stream of loyal readers. This is a good opportunity for you to generate some revenue to reward your blogging efforts. In the dot com era, advertising was one major stream of revenue that kept Web sites alive. However, with the burst of the dot com bubble, looking for advertisers is getting more and more difficult.

Instead of looking for advertisers to buy ads on your site (which is not an easy thing unless you have a very famous blog), I will show you how you can easily make some money using Google's AdSense and Amazon.com's Associates program.

Amazon.com Associates

A great way to generate revenue for your blog is to become an Amazon.com associate. You can earn revenue by promoting products sold by Amazon.com, simply by advertising the products on your blog.

To learn more about becoming an Amazon.com associate, go to `http://www.amazon.com/associates`. To register as an Amazon.com associate, click the **Join now** button to register for a free Amazon.com account (see Figure 6.1).

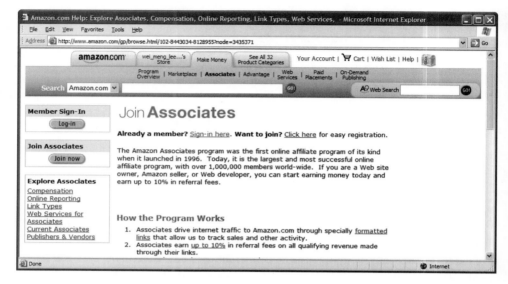

Figure 6.1: Joining as an Amazon.com Associate.

You will be asked to supply some personal information as well as your Web site. When your application is approved, you can log in to Amazon.com using the **Log-in** button shown in Figure 6.1.

Amazon.com Associates Central is the page that allows you to monitor your earnings from Amazon.com. But before you look at your earnings (which is not applicable if you have just joined), you need to create the necessary links to point to the products that you want to promote on your blog.

To create links to the products to promote, follow these steps:

1. At the Amazon.com Associates Central site, click the **Build Links** link, as seen on the left of Figure 6.2.

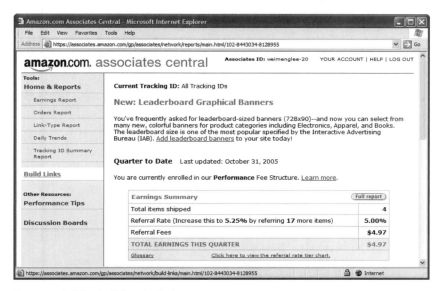

Figure 6.2: Building the Links to the Products.

2. You have several options to build your link. For this example, let's build a simple link to point to a single item—specifically, a book. Click the **Build links** button (see Figure 6.3).

Figure 6.3: Selecting the Items To Link To.

3. You can search for the product you want to link to by specifying its keyword, or more accurately, its ASIN/ISBN number. In Figure 6.4, I have specified the ISBN number of a book (*Harry Potter and the Half-Blood Prince*). Click the **Go** button to search for the book.

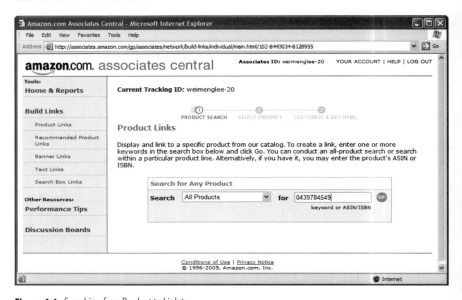

Figure 6.4: Searching for a Product to Link to.

4. Figure 6.5 shows the result of the search. Since there is only a single result for the search, first click the **Get HTML** button to get the HTML code for linking to the item.

Figure 6.5: Results of the Search.

5. Figure 6.6 shows a preview of how the link will look. To paste the link onto your blog, click the **Highlight HTML** button and then press Ctrl-C to copy the HTML code to clipboard.

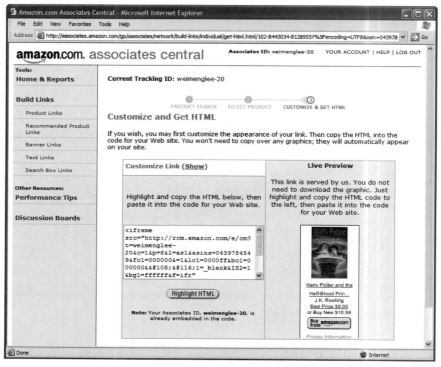

Figure 6.6: Previewing the Link.

6. Go to the Blogger Dashboard and click the **Template**⇨ **Edit current** tab (see Figure 6.7).

Figure 6.7: Inserting the HTML Code into Your Blog Template.

7. Paste the HTML code that you have just copied into the HTML for the template. Specifically, the HTML code is pasted just after the **About** category in the sidebar.

    The following code in bold shows that I have added in a <h2> element and embedded the Amazon.com-generated code with a <center> element.

```
...
<!-- Begin #sidebar -->
<div id="sidebar">
  <center>
    <a href="<$BlogSiteFeedUrl$>" title="Atom feed"><img src="http://
⮑photos1.blogger.com/blogger/4381/1690/1600/atom_icon2.gif" /></a>
  </center>
```

```
<h2 class="sidebar-title">About</h2>

<p><$BlogDescription$></p>

<!-- Begin #profile-container -->

<$BlogMemberProfile$>

<!-- End #profile -->

<MainOrArchivePage>

  <h2 class="sidebar-title">Recommended Books</h2>
    <center>
    <iframe src="http://rcm.amazon.com/e/cm?t=weimenglee-20&o=1&p=8
&l=as1&asins=0439784549&fc1=000000&=1&lc1=0000ff&bc1=000000&&
#108;&#116;1=_blank&IS2=1&bg1=ffffff&f=ifr" style="width:120px;
height:240px;" scrolling="no" marginwidth="0" marginheight="0"
frameborder="0"></iframe>
    </center>

  <h2 class="sidebar-title">Links</h2>
    <ul>
      <li><a href="http://news.google.com/">Google News</a></li>
      <li><a href="http://http://maps.google.com/">Google Maps</a></li>
      <li><a href="http://www.amazon.com/">Amazon.com</a></li>
    </ul>
</MainOrArchivePage>

    <h2 class="sidebar-title">Previous</h2>
...
```

Listing 6.1: Embedding HTML Code in the Blog Template.

8. Click the **Save Template Changes** button and then the **Republish** button to republish the blog. Refresh your blog again and the sidebar will now contain the link to Amazon.com (see Figure 6.8).

Figure 6.8: Viewing the Amazon.com Product Link in Your Blog.

9. When you click the book cover, you will be redirected to Amazon.com site (see Figure 6.9). You will earn a sales commission when a visitor of your blog purchases an item (even if it's not the item you directly point to).

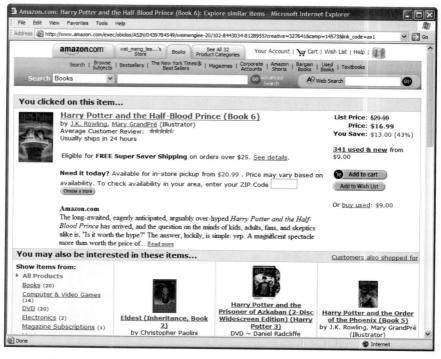

Figure 6.9: Viewing the Product in Amazon.com.

AdSense for Content

AdSense is one of the most innovative ways for you to make some money using your blog. By displaying ads (from Google) on your blog, you will be paid every time your readers click the advertisements on your blog. Best of all, the advertisements on your blog are automatically selected based on the content of your blog, ensuring that they always stay updated and relevant to your readers.

Applying for AdSense is easy. Simply go to the **Template⇨AdSense** tab and fill in your particulars (see Figure 6.10).

Figure 6.10: Applying for AdSense in Blogger.

Once you have signed up for AdSense, you can return to the **Template**⇨**AdSense** tab. Once you have signed in, you will notice a WYSIWYG interface to customize AdSense right inside Blogger.

Alternatively, you can also apply for AdSense at `http://www.google.com/adsense/` (see Figure 6.11).

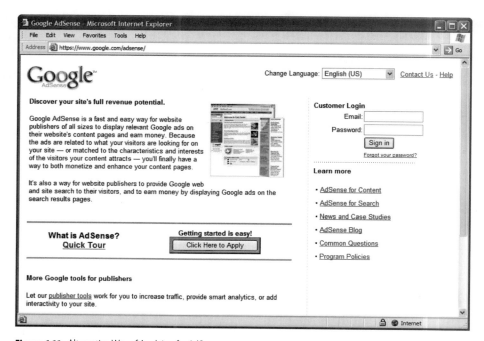

Figure 6.11: Alternative Way of Applying for AdSense.

Once you have applied for AdSense, it will take about two to three days for your application to be approved. Essentially, Google wants to ensure that your blog is the right candidate for displaying advertisements. Once your application is approved, you will receive an e-mail notifying you of the outcome of your application and how you can proceed.

Here's how to use AdSense:

1. Log in to the AdSense page as shown in Figure 6.11. The first thing you need to do is to read AdSense's terms and conditions. Scroll to the bottom of the page, check the agreement check box and click **I Accept** (if you agree to the terms).

2. You will be brought to the **Reports** tab (see Figure 6.12). This will be the page for you to check your earnings for AdSense for Content and AdSense for Search (described in the next section). If you are logged in for the first time, click the **Click here for details** link to set up your payment options.

Figure 6.12: Logging in to AdSense.

3. For now, let's look at how you can generate the ads to display on your blog.
    Click the **AdSense for Content** tab (see Figure 6.13). There are a number of
    options available. For most of them, you will accept the default options.

Figure 6.13: Specifying Ad Layout.

4. Select the size of the advertisement as **120 x 240 Vertical Banner**. You can view the different types of advertisements available by clicking the **View Samples** link. Figure 6.14 shows some of the sample sizes.

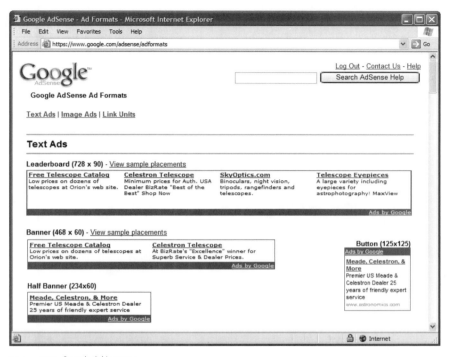

Figure 6.14: Sample Ad Layouts.

5. Once you have selected the size of the advertisement, scroll down the page and you can see a large text box containing JavaScript code (see Figure 6.15). This code is dynamically generated based on your selection in this page. Click the text box and you will notice that the entire block of code is selected. Press Ctrl-C to copy the block of code to clipboard.

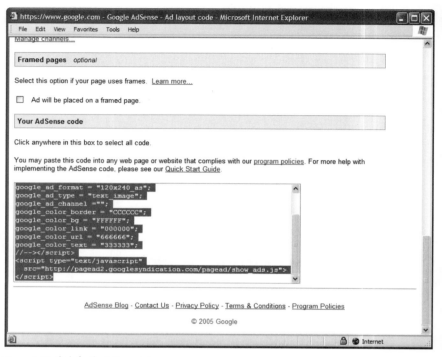

Figure 6.15: Code for the AdSense Ads.

6. Log in to your Blogger account and go to the **Template**⇨ **Edit current** tab. Paste (press Ctrl-V) the AdSense code into the template as shown in Figure 6.16. You are essentially displaying the AdSense advertisements in the sidebar (just after the Blogger logo). Click the **Save Template Changes** button and then the **Republish** button to republish the blog.

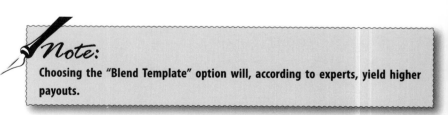

Note:

Choosing the "Blend Template" option will, according to experts, yield higher payouts.

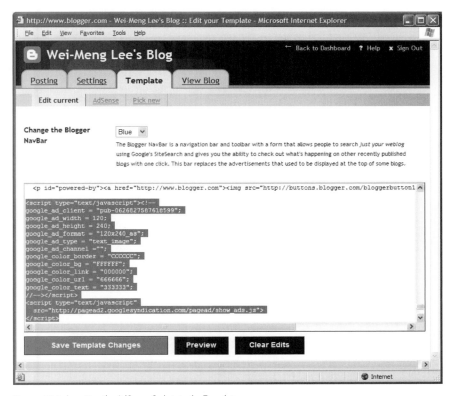

Figure 6.16: Inserting the AdSense Code into the Template.

7. Refresh your blog in the Web browser and you will now see the AdSense advertisements, as shown in Figure 6.17.

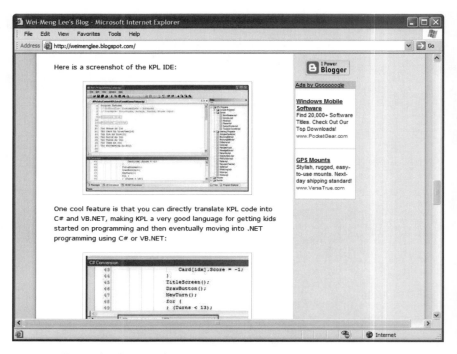

Figure 6.17: Viewing the Ads on Your Blog.

Do not click the advertisements on your own blog. Doing so violates the AdSense agreement and will result in your AdSense accouht being suspended.

AdSense for Search

Besides displaying advertisements on your blog, you can also add Google Search to your blog. This allows your readers to quickly search the Internet (or within your blog) using Google Search.

Just follow these steps:

1. As shown in Figure 6.18, select the **AdSense for Search** tab to generate the necessary code.

Figure 6.18: Generating Code for Google Search.

2. Scroll down the page and change the width of the Google Search box (see Figure 6.19) so that you will fit the Google Search box to the sidebar of your blog. Change the length of the text box to 20 characters and check the following options:

    ▶ **Google logo above text box**

    ▶ **Search button below text box**

3. Click the **Update Code** button to generate the code for the Google Search box.

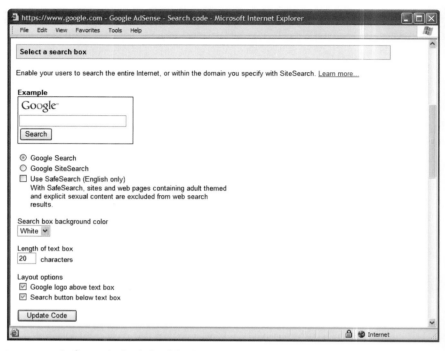

Figure 6.19: Configuring the Google Search Box Options.

4. The code for displaying the Google Search box is displayed at the bottom of the page (see Figure 6.20). Click the code and press Ctrl-C to copy the code into the clipboard.

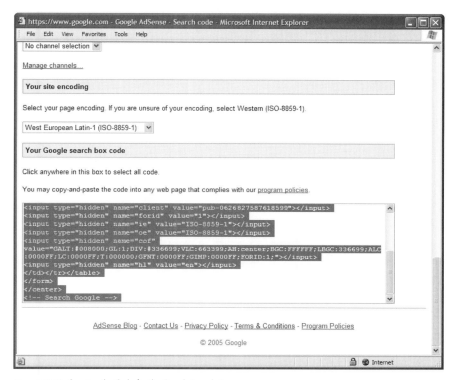

Figure 6.20: Copying the Code for the Google Search Box.

5. In Blogger's **Template⇨ Edit current** tab, insert the Google Search code as shown in Figure 6.21. Essentially, you are adding the search box after the AdSense advertisements. Click the **Save Template Changes** button and then the **Republish** button to republish the blog.

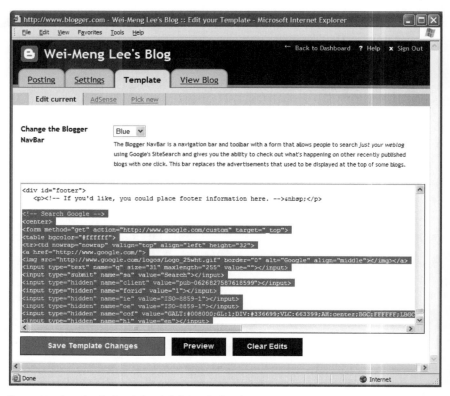

Figure 6.21: Inserting the Google Search Code into the Template.

6.   You will now be able to see the Google Search box in the sidebar of your blog
     (see Figure 6.22). Enter some search query (such as "Pocket PC") and then
     click **Search**.

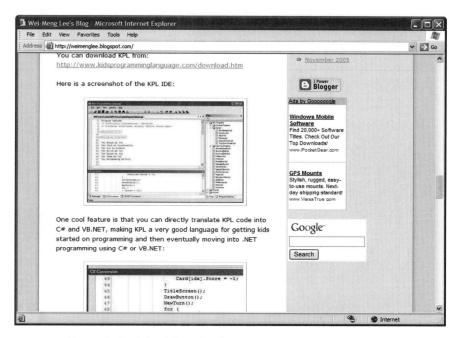

Figure 6.22: Viewing the Google Search Box in Your Blog.

7. You will see the search result together with some advertisements, as seen in Figure 6.23. If the user clicks on the advertisements, you will be paid.

Figure 6.23: Search Results Returned with Ads.

Summary

In this chapter, you have seen that it is quite easy to generate revenue with your blog. All you need is to do is focus on making your blog interesting so that you have a wide readership. AdSense works pretty much by itself and there is no need for you to worry about ad rotation. However, you can fine tune your blog so that AdSense is able to select the most relevant ads, thereby increasing your potential revenue. A discussion of this is beyond the scope of this book, but I suggest you take a look at the AdSense Web site to get a better idea of how to do this. For Amazon.com, be sure to change the links to the items often, so that the products featured can be as timely and relevant as possible.

Advanced Concepts

Chapter 7

Enhancing Your Blog

If you have been following the first few chapters, you should now have your blog up and running. This chapter shows you how to enhance your blog by adding a site counter to track your readership. You will also learn how to archive your blog when you post more frequently. For those of you who have your own Web hosting, you will learn how to publish your blog to your own server, instead of Blogger's.

Adding Site Counters

Suppose you have published your blog and told your friends to visit it. You may even have advertised your blog on some newsgroups. But how do you know if there are people visiting your blog? How do you know if all your efforts in keeping your blog updated are appreciated by readers? The best way to know the answer is to add a *site counter* to your blog so that you have a good idea of the number of readers you have. Today, site counters do much more than simply display a number indicating the total number of visitors. They also contain a wealth of detailed information about your visitors. They allow you to analyze your blog readership, which is especially important if you want to make money from your blog.

To add a site counter to your blog, you can simply make use of the services provided by site counter providers. Best of all, most of these site counter providers offer free services for basic functionalities, but you can pay a nominal amount for advanced services if you need to.

One of the site counter providers that I use is StatCounter (`http://www.statcounter.com/`). StatCounter is a reliable and invisible Web tracker, a highly configurable hit counter, and a real-time detailed Web stats provider. To use StatCounter, simply insert a piece of code into your blog and you will be able to analyze and monitor all the visitors to your blog in real-time.

Here's how to use StatCounter:

1. Go to `http://my.statcounter.com/register.php` and register for a free account.

2. Once your account has been created, you will see the screen shown in Figure 7.1. To use StatCounter to monitor your blog, click the **ADD A STATCOUNTER PROJECT** icon.

Figure 7.1: Creating a New StatCounter Project.

3. Specify the type of project you want to create. To create a site counter for your blog, select the **STANDARD STATCOUNTER PROJECT** radio button and click the **Next** button (see Figure 7.2).

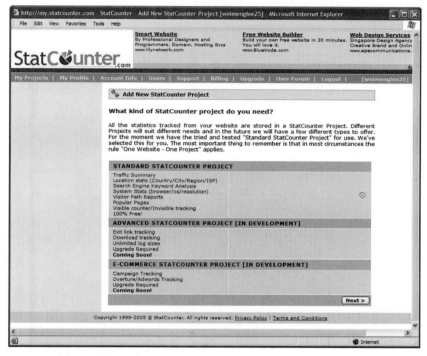

Figure 7.2: Selecting the Type of Project.

4. Supply the detailed information for your blog (see Figure 7.3) and click the
   Next button.

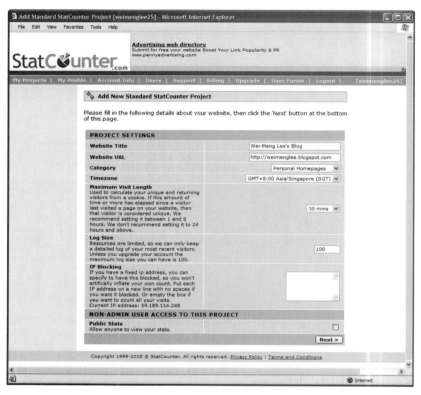

Figure 7.3: Entering Details of Your Blog.

5. Once your project is created, you need to configure the site counter for use. Click the **CONFIGURE & INSTALL CODE** icon (see Figure 7.4) to proceed.

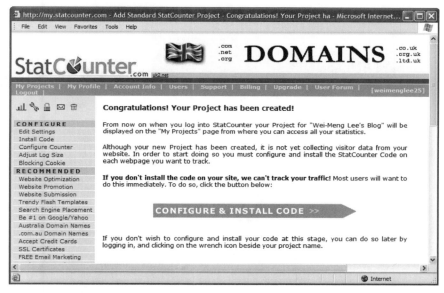

Figure 7.4: Configuring the Project.

6. You will first need to select the type of counter you want. Select the **VISIBLE COUNTER** radio button and click the **Next** button (see Figure 7.5).

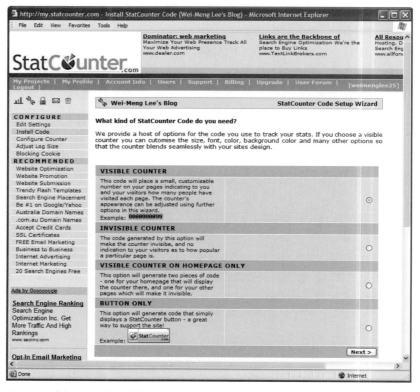

Figure 7.5: Selecting the Type of Counter.

7. You can select how the site counter registers each visit (see Figure 7.6). For our example, select the **Every Pageload** radio button so that every time your blog is loaded, the counter increases by one (regardless if this is a page refresh by the same user). Also, you have the option to change the starting number of your site counter. Click the **Next** button.

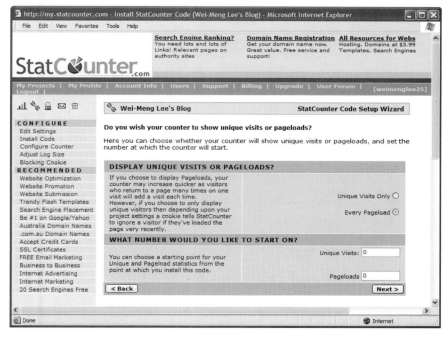

Figure 7.6: Selecting How the Site Counter Registers a Hit.

8. You can choose to display your site counter as an image, or simply as text. For our example, select the **Counter Image** radio button (see Figure 7.7) and click the **Next** button.

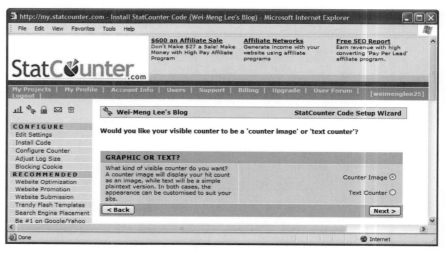

Figure 7.7: Selecting Either Image or Text for Your Site Counter.

9. The default number of digits used for your site counter is eight. You can also change its color (see Figure 7.8) and preview how your site counter will look. Click the **Next** button.

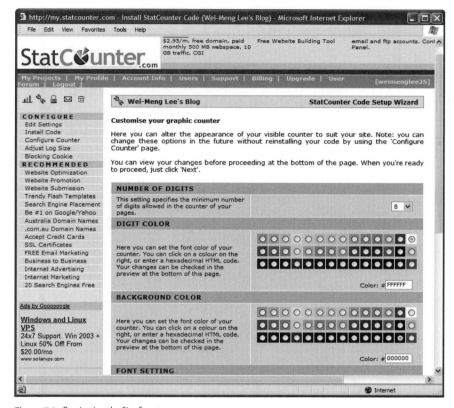

Figure 7.8: Previewing the Site Counter.

10. The next screen will let you indicate any specific requirements of your site, such as whether your site uses frames, or if you need to ensure that your site is W3C or XHTML compliant. Check the **No, my website does not use frames option** (see Figure 7.9) and click the **Next** button.

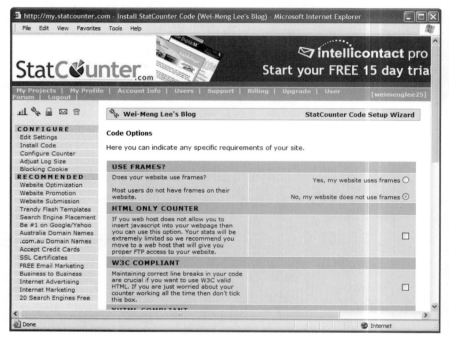

Figure 7.9: Specifying Additional Requirements for Your Site.

11. Since we want to install the site counter manually for this example, check the default **No, I want the default install guide** option (see Figure 7.10) and click the **Next** button.

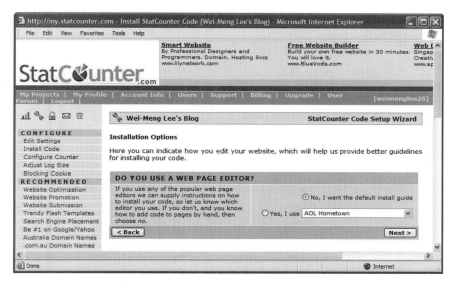

Figure 7.10: Selecting Install Options.

12. The page shown in Figure 7.11 contains the code that you need to insert into your blog. Highlight the code shown in the text box and press Ctrl-C to copy it to the clipboard.

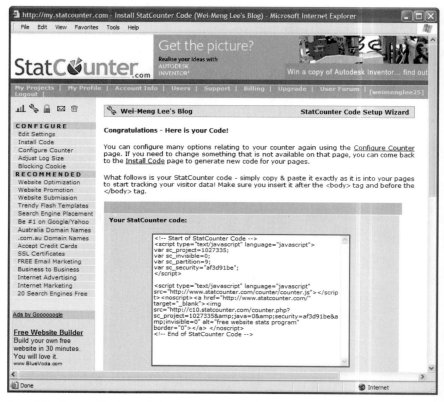

Figure 7.11: Generated Site Counter Code.

13. You will insert the site counter at the bottom of your blog, so you need to modify the template of your blog. In the **Template⇨ Edit current** tab, scroll to the bottom of the text box and insert the site counter code (press Ctrl-V) at the location shown in Figure 7.12.

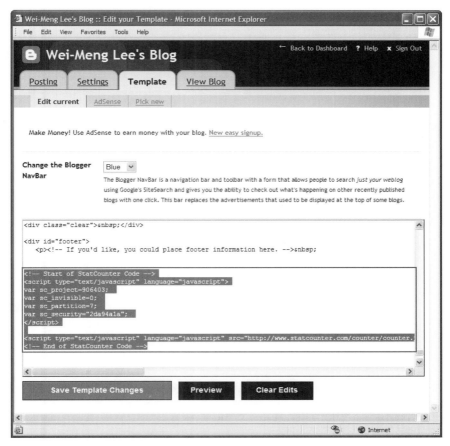

Figure 7.12: Inserting the Site Counter Code into Your Blog Template.

14. Click the **Save Template Changes** button to save the changes and then click the **Republish** button to republish the site.

15. Refresh your blog and the site counter should now appear at the bottom of the page (see Figure 7.13). Refresh your page (press F5) and you will see that the counter increases.

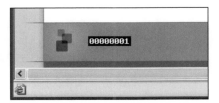

Figure 7.13: Viewing the Site Counter in Action.

Viewing Site Counter Information

Once your site counter is up and running, it is time to find out more about the demography of your visitors. Follow these steps:

1. Log in to StatCounter and you will see the project name that you have created in the last section, as shown in Figure 7.14. Click the project name to view detailed information about your site.

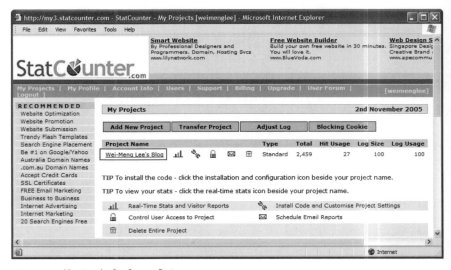

Figure 7.14: Viewing the StatCounter Project.

2. You will first see a summary of your site traffic for the past eight days (see Figure 7.15). You will be able to see the total number of page loads, unique visitors, and returning visitors. There is also a list of statistics (on the left of the page under the header **STATISTICS**).

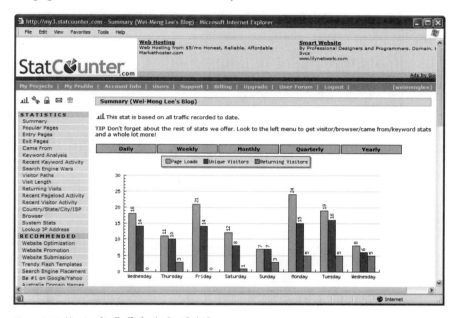

Figure 7.15: Viewing Site Traffic for the Past Eight Days.

3. Figure 7.16 shows the **Recent Pageload Activity** option, which shows the detailed information of your visitors. You will be able to see where your visitors come from, what OS and Web browser they are using, as well as the referrer link.

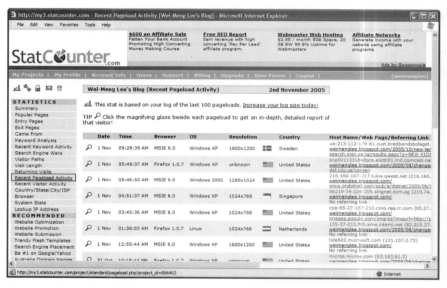

Figure 7.16: Viewing Detailed Pageload Activity.

4. The **Referring Link** column is a good way to know where your visitors are coming from. For example, Figure 7.17 shows that a particular user located one of my postings on my blog through MSN search.

Country	Host Name/Web Page/Referring Link
United States	ip68-225-247-66.oc.oc.cox.net (68.225.247.66) weimenglee.blogspot.com/2005/10/whats-new-in-windows-mobile-50.html search.msn.com/results.aspx?q=what's new in windows mobile 5.0%3F&first=11&FORM=PERE

Figure 7.17: Viewing the Referring Link Information.

5. Click the **Return Visits** option to display a pie chart showing the details of returning visitors (see Figure 7.18).

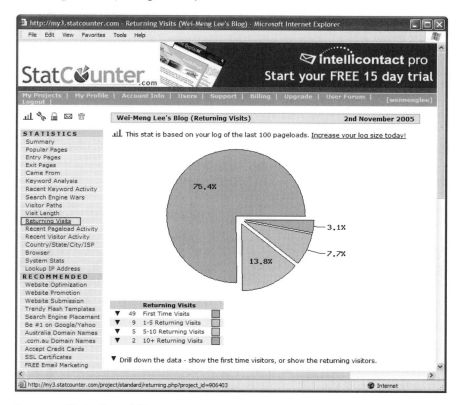

Figure 7.18: Viewing Types of Visits.

Archiving Blogs

Over time, your blog page will contain more and more postings. As the number of postings increases, the page will get lengthier and take much longer to load. By default, Blogger will archive your postings on a monthly basis. That is, you will see the **Archives** section in your sidebar showing links to pages that contain your postings for a particular month (see Figure 7.19).

Figure 7.19: Archives Section in Your Blog Sidebar.

However, if you blog frequently, you should archive your blog more often. You can specify the archive frequency in the **Settings**⇨ **Archiving** tab (see Figure 7.20). You can archive **Daily**, **Weekly**, **Monthly**, or specify no archive at all.

Figure 7.20: Specifying the Archive Frequency.

Click the **Save Settings** button to save the changes and then click the **Republish** button to republish the entire blog.

Hosting Your Own Blog

Up to this point, you have been using the hosting service offered by Blogger to host your blog. While this service is free, there is a limit on the disk space available for your blog (and that limits the number of pictures you can upload to Blogger). Also, you are forced to use the domain name "blogspot.com" for your blog. For people who already have their own Web site, it makes more sense for them to host their blog on their own server (or the hosting company's) and have their own desired URL for their blog.

Here's how to publish your blog on your own dedicated server using FTP.

1. Log in to Blogger and in the **Settings** ⇨ **Publishing** tab, click the **FTP** link (see Figure 7.21) so that you can configure the FTP settings of your hosting server.

Figure 7.21: Selecting FTP for Publishing Your Blog.

2.   The screen shown in Figure 7.22 appears. Here is where you will specify the FTP settings of your hosting server (see Figure 7.22).

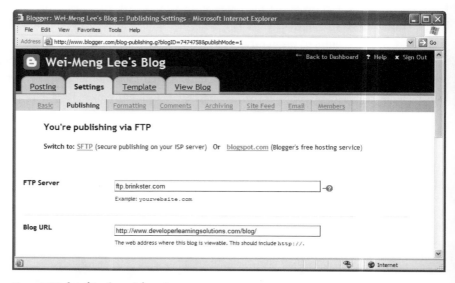

Figure 7.22: Specifying Server Information.

Table 7.1 shows the settings that you need to fill in.

Setting	Example
FTP Server	ftp.brinkster.com
Blog URL	http://www.developerlearningsolutions.com/blog/
FTP Path	webroot/blog/
Blog Filename	index.html. If this file already exists on your server in the path entered above, it will be overwritten. Be sure to back it up.
FTP Username	FTP Password; Username and Password are optional. If you leave them blank, you will be asked to enter them when you publish your blog.
Notify Weblogs.com	Yes/No

Table 7.1: Required FTP Server Information.

3. The settings in Table 7.1 show that I have a hosting account with Brinkster. com. The root path for my FTP account is **webroot** (this directory is where I store my HTML files for my company Web site at http://www.developerl earningsolutions.com). I have created a new directory under **webroot** and named it blog to store my blog. And so in the **FTP Path** setting, I specified webroot/blog. The **Blog Filename** setting is the name of the file that will contain your blog postings.

4. When done, click **Save Settings**. You need to click the **Republish** button so that your blog can now be published to your server (see Figure 7.23).

Figure 7.23: Republishing Your Blog to Your Server.

5. To view your newly published blog, go to the URL that you specified earlier in the **Blog URL** setting. You should now be able to view your blog (see Figure 7.24).

Figure 7.24: Viewing the Blog at the New URL.

Archiving

When you are publishing your blog to another server other than Blogger's, you also need to specify additional settings for your archived blog. In particular, you need to go to the **Settings⇨Archiving** tab and fill in the three pieces of information shown at the bottom of Figure 7.25.

Figure 7.25: Settings for Blog Archives.

Figure 7.25 shows that my archived blog will be published to the Webroot/blog folder and the file names will end with **developerlearningsolutions_archive.html**. For example, a page archived in September will have this file name: 2005_09_01_developerlearningsolu tions_archive.html.

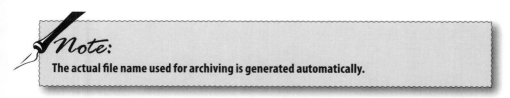

Note:

The actual file name used for archiving is generated automatically.

Summary

In this chapter, you have seen how to add a site counter to your page so that you can view detailed information about your readers. Knowing your target readers is useful if you want to make money using your blog. In addition, you also learned how to archive your blog and publish it to your own server.

Chapter 8

Mobile Blogging

Up to this point, you have all the required information to create a nice and informative blog. You have seen how to add postings to your blog using the Post Editor, as well as how to use e-mail for posting. All these methods make blogging a much simplified process, but they all require the use of a computer. What if you come across some beautiful scenery and want to capture the moment using your camera-equipped mobile phone and then share it with your blog readers? Fortunately, Blogger allows you to post to your blog using either MMS (Multimedia Messaging Service) or e-mails on your mobile phone. In this chapter, you will learn how to use Blogger Mobile for mobile blogging.

Using Blogger Mobile

To use Blogger Mobile, you need a mobile device that allows you to send MMS messages or e-mails. Simply send an e-mail (or MMS) containing the text of your post (and images, if any) to go@blogger.com. Figure 8.1 shows an e-mail containing an image attachment created in Pocket PC.

Note:

For mobile blogging using MMS, Blogger Mobile currently supports only the following carriers in the US: Sprint, Verizon, T-Mobile, and AT&T/Cingular.

> ## Tech Tip:
>
> **If your Pocket PC contains a built-in camera, it is a good idea to use Blogger Mobile for mobile blogging, as you can take pictures with it and then blog the pictures directly by sending an e-mail or MMS.**

Figure 8.1: Sending an E-mail in Pocket PC.

After the e-mail is sent, you will receive an acknowledgement e-mail (see Figure 8.2) from Blogger Mobile, informing you of the creation of your blog (if you are using Blogger Mobile for the first time). This acknowledgement e-mail will contain the URL of your newly created blog, as well as a code for you to claim your blog. Meanwhile, you can continue blogging by sending e-mails to go@blogger.com.

Figure 8.2: E-mail Acknowledgement from Blogger.

When you have a chance to use a computer, you can claim your blog by following these steps:

1. Go to `http://go.blogger.com`. In the **Claim token** field (see Figure 8.3), enter the code shown in the acknowledgement e-mail, and then click the **Continue** button.

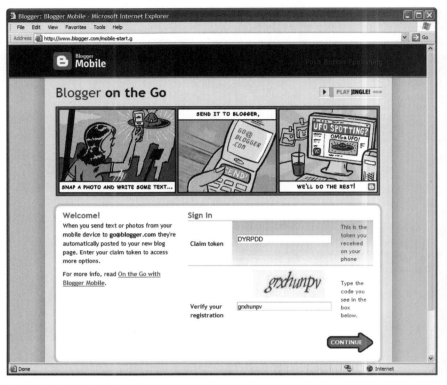

Figure 8.3: Claiming Your Blog.

2. If you have entered the code correctly, you will see the **Mobile Blog Found** page (shown in Figure 8.4). If you already have a Blogger account, log in now. If not, you can set up a new account. For now, sign in to the Blogger account you have been using for the past few chapters, and click the **Continue** button.

Figure 8.4: Locating the Mobile Blog.

3. If you have logged in to your current Blogger account, you will see the page shown in Figure 8.5. You have the option to transfer the postings in the mobile blog to your existing Blogger account (**Wei-Meng Lee's Blog**, in my case), or you can keep sending your mobile posts to the one Blogger Mobile has created for you—http://hubnet24.blosgpot.com (this URL is randomly generated for each new Blogger Mobile user).

Figure 8.5: Options to Transfer the Mobile Blog to Your Existing Blogger Account.

4. If you use the default blog that Blogger Mobile has created for you, you can visit your blog by clicking the `http://hubnet24.blosgpot.com` link. You can see your blog now (see Figure 8.6).

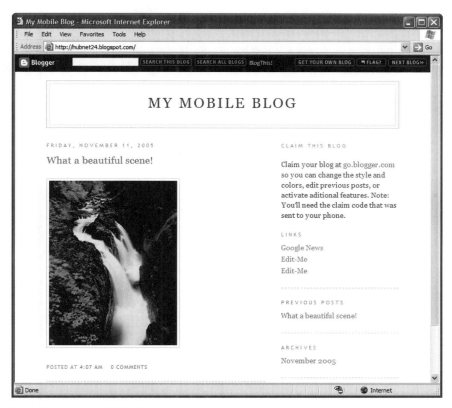

Figure 8.6: Viewing the Mobile Blog.

Tech Tip:
To customize the look of your new blog, click the **Set up your account** link shown previously in Figure 8.4.

5. If you have chosen the **Switch to Wei-Meng Lee's blog** option in Figure 8.5, you will see the screen shown in Figure 8.7. Click the **Finish** button to continue.

Figure 8.7: Transfer Mobile Blog to Existing Blogger Account Complete.

6. To view the blog that is merged with your existing blog, go to your existing blog and you will see the new entry (see Figure 8.8).

Figure 8.8: Viewing Your Blog.

7. From now on, whenever you post to your blog using Blogger Mobile, your acknowledgment e-mail will indicate the URL of your mobile blog, as shown in Figure 8.9.

Figure 8.9: Acknowledgement E-mails from Blogger Mobile.

Configuring Blogger Mobile

If you want to change the blog that your mobile device is currently posting to, you can modify the settings in the Dashboard. In the sidebar of the Dashboard, you will see the section named **Mobile Devices**. Figure 8.10 shows that e-mails sent from `wei_meng_lee@hotmail.com` are sent to my blog (**Wei-Meng Lee's Blog**).

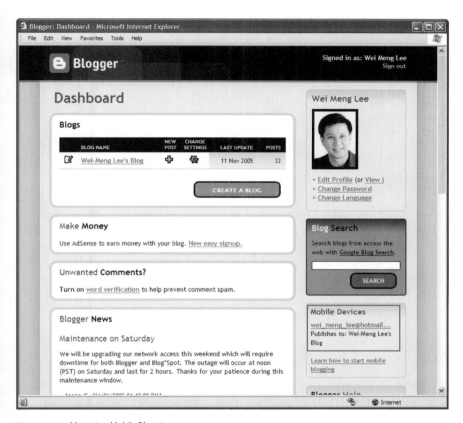

Figure 8.10: Managing Mobile Blogging.

To change the association, you can click the e-mail address. You can delete this blog by clicking the **Delete This Device** button. If you have multiple blogs, you can also select the blog to post to. Click the **Save Settings** button to save the changes (see Figure 8.11).

Figure 8.11: Changing Device Settings.

Tech Tip:

The main difference between Blogger Mobile and Mail-to-Blogger (discussed in Chapter 3) is that Blogger Mobile automatically creates a new blog for you the first time you use it; you do not need a computer in order to post your blog.

For more information on Blogger Mobile, checkout the FAQ at `http://help.blogger.com/bin/answer.py?answer=1137`.

Tech Tip.

Another way to blog while you're out and about is to use Audioblogger (`http://www.audioblogger.com/`). Audioblogger.com is a new service that allows users to call a phone number to record and send a voice post (mp3) to their blog.

Summary

In this chapter, you have seen how you can post to your blog using Blogger Mobile. Blogger Mobile is a useful service provided by Blogger, because it allows you to blog from the convenience of your mobile device, without the need for a computer.

Did you know?

There is another way to blog while you're out and about. You can use Audioblogger (available at `http://www.audioblogger.com/`). This is a new service that allows users to call a phone number to record and send a voice post (mp3) to their blog.

Chapter 9

Google Reader

As mentioned in Chapter 1, you can use a newsreader to aggregate all the blogs that interest you. While a Windows-based newsreader offers you a lot of features and flexibility, its limitations quickly become apparent when you move from one computer to another. Blogs that you subscribed to on one computer must be subscribed to again on the other computer. A better solution would be to use a Web-based newsreader, so that wherever you go, your subscribed blogs will always be there.

This chapter shows you how to use the new Google Reader, which at the time of writing is still in beta. The Google Reader is located at: `http://www.google.com/reader`.

Logging in to Google Reader

To use the Google Reader, you can use your Gmail account or any other Google service accounts. If you do not have any Google account, you can click on the **Create an account now** link (see Figure 9.1).

Figure 9.1: To Use Google Reader, You Need a Google Account.

Once you have logged in or created a new Google account service, you will be redirected to the Google Reader (see Figure 9.2).

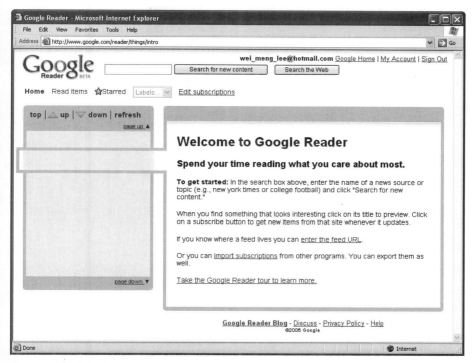

Figure 9.2: Google Reader.

Subscribing to Blogs

The easiest way to subscribe to a blog in Google Reader is to use the search function. For example, if I want to subscribe to the blog at Engadget.com, I would type `engadget` into the text box and then click the **Search for new content** button (see Figure 9.3). Google Reader will return a list of matching blogs. To subscribe to a blog, simply click the **Subscribe** button.

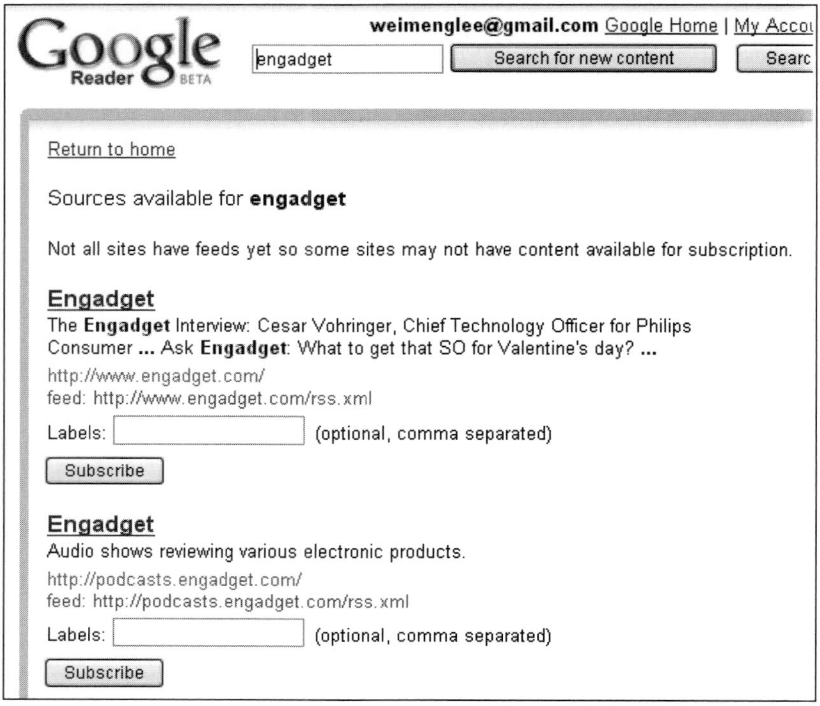

Figure 9.3: Subscribing to a Blog.

You can subscribe to as many blogs as you like in this page. Once a blog subscription is successful, click the **Return to home** link at the top of the screen to return to the main screen of Google Reader.

Reading Blog Postings

Figure 9.4 shows Google Reader displaying postings from the various blogs that I have subscribed to. Notice that Google Reader will mix all the postings from the different blogs and display their titles in a list. Unread postings are displayed in bold. By default, all read and unread items are displayed in the list. You can choose to hide read postings by clicking the **hidden** link (located at the bottom of the list).

Figure 9.4: Reading Blog Postings.

At the top right corner of the posting, you can also select the **BlogThis!** option (see Figure 9.5) from the drop-down menu to blog the posting directly onto your Blogger blog.

Figure 9.5: Blogging a Post Directly onto Blogger.

You will be asked to sign in to Blogger first, and then you can modify the posting and publish it to your blog (see Figure 9.6).

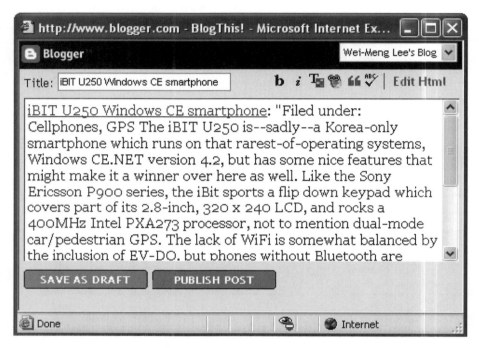

Figure 9.6: Using the BlogThis! Option.

Attaching Labels to Blog Postings

Often, you want to retrieve postings that you have read previously. For example, you might have read a posting about some new smart phones and then wish to retrieve the posting a few days later. But what if you cannot remember where you have read the posting?

One good way to help you remember interesting posts is to attach labels to them. This is easy. Simply scroll to the bottom of a post and click the **edit** link displayed next to the **Your labels** text. You can now enter a label to attach to this post. Click the **Save** button to save the label (see Figure 9.7).

Tech Tip:

Google has released a new feature that allows users to share what they read with their blog audience. Check it out at `http://googlereader.blogspot.com/2006/03/reader-learns-to-share.html`.

Your labels: **cancel**

`smartphone`

Separate labels by commas

[Save] [Cancel]

Figure 9.7: Attaching a Label to a Post.

If you wish to retrieve all the postings that have the "smartphone" label, simply select a label from the drop-down menu at the top of the page, as shown in Figure 9.8.

Figure 9.8: Using the Labels Feature.

Alternatively, you can press "**g**" then "**l**" to bring up the label selector (see Figure 9.9).

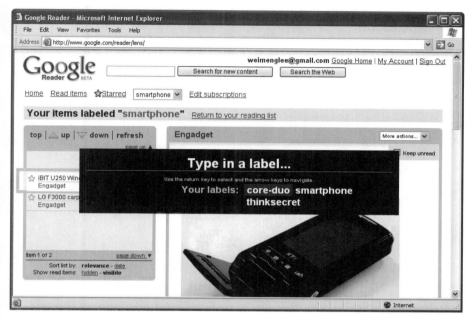

Figure 9.9: Using Keyboard Shortcuts to Bring Up the Label Selector.

Starring Blog Postings

Besides attaching labels to a post, you can also "star" a blog posting for later perusal. This feature is useful if you come across an interesting post but do not have time to read it now. To "star" a post, simply click the star icon next to a post (see Figure 9.10).

Figure 9.10: Starring Posts.

To read all starred postings, click the **Starred** link at the top of the page (see Figure 9.11).

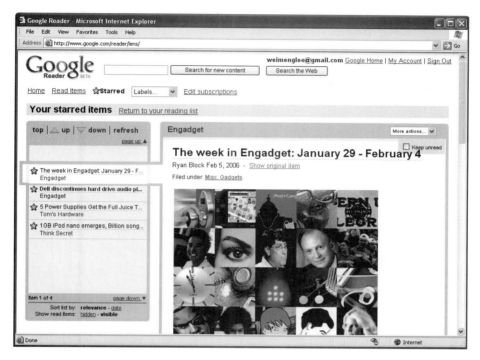

Figure 9.11: Reading All Starred Postings.

Managing Your Subscriptions

You can manage your subscriptions by clicking the **Edit subscriptions** link at the top of the page. Once you click the link, a list of the subscribed blogs appears (see Figure 9.12). You can click on a blog name to read all the postings in the selected blog.

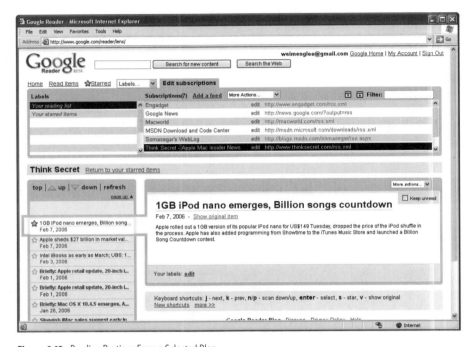

Figure 9.12: Reading Postings From a Selected Blog.

You can also click the **edit** link of a blog to add labels to the blog or to unsubscribe from the blog (see Figure 9.13).

Figure 9.13: Attaching Labels to a Blog.

Tech Tip:

When you unsubscribe a blog, you need to log out and log in again in order for the blog to be removed from the list.

Importing Subscriptions

To import subscriptions from another newsreader, you can click the drop-down menu (see Figure 9.14) and select **Import subscriptions**.

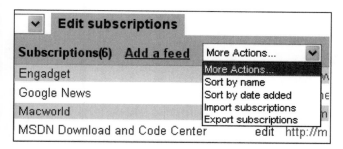

Figure 9.14: Importing a Subscription.

You will then be asked for the name of the OPML file containing the list of subscriptions (see Figure 9.15).

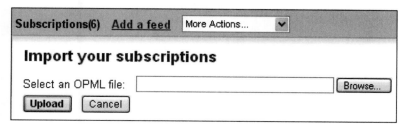

Figure 9.15: Selecting an OPML File for Import.

Exporting Your Subscriptions

You can also export your current subscriptions in Google Reader as an OPML file. Select **Export subscriptions** in the drop-down list and an OPML XML document will be generated (see Figure 9.16). You can save this document and share it with your friends.

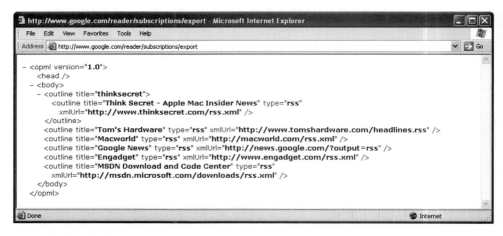

Figure 9.16: Exporting Your Subscriptions.

Adding a Feed Manually

To subscribe to a blog manually, click the **Add a feed** link (see Figure 9.17) and enter the URL of the blog.

Figure 9.17: Subscribing to a Blog Manually.

For example, enter the following feed URL: `http://weimenglee.blogspot.com/atom.xml`. Click the **Preview** button. You will be able to preview the blog and if you like what you see, click the **Subscribe** button to subscribe to the blog (see Figure 9.18).

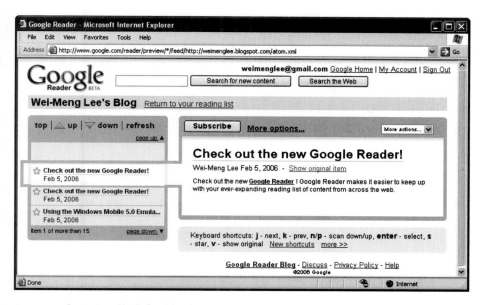

Figure 9.18: Previewing a Blog Before Subscribing.

Summary

In this chapter, you have seen the features available in the new Google Reader. You learned how to subscribe to blogs, attach labels, "star" blogs for later reading, and how to manage your subscriptions. As the Google Reader is still in beta, expect to see more features by the time you read this. In the meantime, check out the Google Reader and you will be amazed by its ease of use.

FREE *Bonus:*

The following bonus chapter is available as a free download when you register your book at www.rationalpress.com (see the last page in this book for instructions):

► **Bonus Chapter: "Using the Blogger Atom API"**

The Blogger Atom API allows programmers to write applications that interact with Blogger programmatically. This bonus chapter shows you how to build your own Blogger client for reading and creating new posts to your blog using the Blogger Atom API.

Extras

Index

S

T

W

Notes

"running - to - now"   until it, to create a tab

Go to: www. blog. com

use g mail name + pwrd

login - emmaemma adams e.g mail. com (gmail address)
p - tightept
Q - cats name -
display: bts (back to school)

① www. blog. com
② g mail name

bookmark Homepage   When create blog, it's going to
   "   dashboard   go to g-mail
DO NOT Shut down - minimize?

new blog - (print out each page) - display name
  ① create the google acct. -   my name
  username - elizabethggie
  pword; cat
don't go to g-mail again - go to www. blogger. com
- Template - mirror
- e-mail an image to your g-mail account. -

Notes

emma.adams.

mail   emanaeuff@blogger.com

set up e-mail addresses from verizon acct.-

can mail to blogger acct.-
subject line is title of post.   emanueff.- can write a
                              - envelope on   blog
blogger will pop it into your blog.

If forget your ass go to settings
do I want picture w/ my comment.

put http://swimming-against-the-stream.blogspot.co
                              is favorites

Notes

Notes

IMPORTANT NOTICE
REGISTER YOUR BOOK

Bonus Materials

Your book refers to valuable material that complements your learning experience. In order to download these materials you will need to register your book at http://www.rationalpress.com.

This bonus material is available after registration:

▶ Bonus chapter: "Using the Blogger Atom API"

Registering your book

To register your book, follow these 7 easy steps:

1. Go to http://www.rationalpress.com.

2. Create an account and login.

3. Click the **My Books** link.

4. Click the **Register New Book** button.

5. Enter the registration number found on the back of the book (Figure A).

6. Confirm registration and view your new book on the virtual bookshelf.

7. Click the spine of the desired book to view the available downloads and resources for the selected book.

Figure A: Back of your book.